AN INTRODUCTION TO Withdrawn
STEINER EDUCATION

AN INTRODUCTION TO
STEINER EDUCATION

The Waldorf School

Francis Edmunds

Sophia Books

Sophia Books
Hillside House, The Square
Forest Row, RH18 5ES

www.rudolfsteinerpress.com

Published by Sophia Books 2004
An imprint of Rudolf Steiner Press

First published in 1979, and reissued 1982, 1986, 1987, 1992.
This edition has been edited, revised and updated by Matthew Barton

A catalogue record for this book is available from the British Library

ISBN 1 85584 172 X

Cover by Andrew Morgan Design
Typeset by DP Photosetting, Aylesbury, Bucks.
Printed and bound in Great Britain by Cromwell Press Limited,
Trowbridge, Wilts.

CONTENTS

Foreword

by Martyn Rawson

It is twenty-five years since Francis Edmunds first published this book, and the Steiner Waldorf Schools movement has changed in many ways in this past quarter century. In view of this it would be justified to ask if such a book is still relevant? What is in many ways more significant is the fact that the world has changed in this time in ways that very few people could have predicted and it is these changes that pose the question: is Steiner Waldorf education itself still relevant?

I started teaching about the time that this book was written. As a visiting student I had experienced Francis at Emerson College. For many of us he was already an almost mythical figure, one who represented an inspiring image of wisdom, genius, mystery and charisma—the very qualities we intuitively associated with the Waldorf Class teacher. As a young man with a young family and a serious task in the world (founding a Waldorf school), a figure like Francis Edmunds was not only an inspiration but a standard one measured oneself against. It is not that one tried to be like him, but one experienced qualities in him that one felt were necessary to cultivate.

There were others among that group of outstanding personalities of his generation from whom we learned and drew courage. Edmunds, though, had a curious aura. He appeared to have a personal following quite unusual in Waldorf circles. Even today I frequently meet people all over the world who almost immediately on hearing of my work in Forest Row tell me of their time at Emerson College and their memories of Francis (Asian people always say Mr Edmunds of course). It seems like it was a golden time for a whole generation of young people who are now leading lights in the international Waldorf School movement. And that seems to be the crucial point—Edmunds and Emerson College brought Waldorf education to the world in a way that was unique. Something of that uniqueness is apparent in this book. Francis Edmunds had the ability to make complex ideas seem comprehensible. He was a great communicator. The ideas underlying Waldorf education can be very hard to grasp. There are many learned books explaining anthroposophy that frankly are barely comprehensible (though few would admit it). Francis lived these ideas and was interested in helping others find their way into them too. This was a great achievement and one that has left a lasting impression on the international Waldorf School movement. Curiously, though, his books have not translated well in German and other languages. For the German ear, Francis seemed lightweight. He wasn't.

Many countries now have their own teacher training programmes, but in those days Emerson was a beacon for Waldorf Education through the English language and as such offered a counterbalance to the German speaking Waldorf centres in Dornach (Switzerland) or Stuttgart. Scandinavia had Järna, the Dutch had Zeist, but the world had Emerson College!

The world but not necessarily Great Britain. Of course many British students did learn to be teachers at Emerson College, but most years they have been in a minority. Emerson College and Francis Edmunds had their greatest influence locally in Forest Row, that quiet backwater in the stockbroker belt south of London, and in the wider world. For many of us in the British Waldorf schools movement, Emerson College was as remote as Dornach or Järna. This curious situation, which had many explanatory factors not relevant here, tells us however something very positive about Francis Edmunds. His understanding and demonstration of

Waldorf education was most brilliant when he addressed what is universally human. It is that dimension of universality that graces both the best in this book and which ultimately makes Waldorf education relevant in a much changed world.

What is the challenge of education in our times? The answer in a word is globalization. This concept includes not only the shift in the global economy away from the industrial Western nations but the cultural impact of the electronic media. Twenty-five years ago the world had a very different economic and political structure. Now the Berlin Wall has fallen and the Soviet Empire has gone, major parts of the Second and Third Worlds, such as India, China and Indonesia, are rapidly developing and becoming the manufacturing powerhouses of the world economy. Multinational consortia and the globalization of world banking and stock markets have replaced national economies (even if politicians are locally in denial). Wealth has been more widely distributed among the nations, though the poor everywhere have got poorer and the rich richer. The cold war has been replaced by the hydra of international terrorism and the rise of fundamentalism, both as a post-colonial backlash but also as an expression of the frustrated aspirations of the citizens of many new nations which, having thrown off their colonial shackles, find themselves under the yoke of home-grown dictatorship—most of which enjoyed Western support at one time or another. But the world really is different after 9.11.

Those global changes are experienced locally in many varied ways. One of the most wide-ranging consequences of the transition in a modern economy from being essentially production-orientated to service-orientated has been the shift in the role of work. Work once involved nearly everybody at some level or other in a self-evident creation of value through the transformation of primary resources into products for the market through the industrial process. In the age of auto-

mation such processes possess the constant tendency to make
human work redundant. The better organized the work
becomes, the fewer people are needed. This has led to mass
unemployment and artificially reduced working hours and
job-sharing, with corresponding social insecurity and alie-
nation. What was to blame was the reduction of the concept
of work exclusively to the activity of production. Work was
what one did to earn a living; it provided social status. What
was described as the natural loss of jobs in the post-industrial
society was in fact a controlled reduction in the length of
working life based on wage-earning linked to production.

The important point is that young people leaving education
and entering the world of work need quite different skills and
abilities. The paradigm shift has led us to readjust our values
and in particular our relationship to the concepts of work and
learning. We used to go to school to prepare ourselves for a
life of working (at least that was the theory and expectation).
The end of the production-based economy and the drastic
reductions in state welfare provision have brought terrible
insecurity and loss of identity, but it has also freed the concept
of work and thus linked it in new ways to learning. *Learning*
began to be recognized as *work* in a life-long learning society
and *work* begins to become a new form of *learning*. Not only
do many forms of work now require us to constantly learn
new skills, use new technologies, above all it means dealing
with knowledge and information.

Where once education was about the acquisition of
knowledge, modern society now requires us to be able to
manage knowledge, and many tasks in the world of work
involve just that. Interestingly the concept of work has now
been expanded to include personal development (to work on
oneself), creativity (to work at solving a problem, creating
new solutions and designs), play, sleep, eating, caring for
one's body (to work-out), feeling and thinking (work it out),

since all these activities lead to the forming of life-habits and personal transformation. Work can take many forms including production, but also including activities such as teamwork, housework, voluntary work. In other words, work has liberated itself from the narrow definition of waged production activity. In doing so it has also re-integrated the two unnatural concepts of work and leisure that was enforced by the production-based society. Leisure was what you did in your free time, i.e. non-earning time. Everything that fosters and leads to personality development can now be recognized as work.

The implications of this change for education are incalculable, inasmuch as education of children and young people was designed ultimately to equip them for their place in the job market.

Take care, for example. Tasks once traditionally done unpaid by women, such as child care, care of the elderly and sick were taken for granted and had little economic value. We now have a new generation of women who no longer wish to assume this burden automatically. And indeed they may actively choose not to, a fact which still causes major domestic and social tensions around the world; it is also a fact which indicates the degree to which men have to acquire social competencies. Now we have to—or better, we wish to—pay for our caring services and these services have become increasingly professionalized and regulated. This has the consequence that most people no longer have the opportunities to learn caring within the family, so parenting for example has to be learned. It is not relevant to make value judgements whether this is a good thing or not—and certainly there are advantages and disadvantages all round. The point is, it is now a fact we have to work consciously with.

We should ask what skills and abilities do people need to acquire to meet the requirements of contemporary society, to be able not simply to cope but to take positive control of their destinies and help shape the society of the future.

Rudolf Steiner formulated this question at the founding of the first Waldorf School in Stuttgart in 1919:

> The parents entrusting their children to this school can only hope and expect that these children will be educated to become competent in life... This makes it necessary for us in founding this school to take our start from pedagogical principles that are rooted in what life in the present demands of us. Our children are to be educated to become people who are prepared for a life that corresponds to these demands, which are ones that can support them, regardless of what social class they come from... Idealism must be at work within the spirit of the pedagogy and methods, but this must be an idealism that has the power to awaken in growing human beings those forces and abilities that they will need for the rest of their lives in order to work competently for their community of contemporaries and to have a livelihood that will sustain them. It would be disastrous if a spirit foreign to life were to prevail in the basic pedagogical views on which the Waldorf School is to be founded.

We have to ask ourselves what a 'spirit foreign to life' might mean in educational terms. Obviously everything that does not foster competence and healthy development would be seen as foreign to human nature. This would include such obviously unproductive experiences as formal learning before the child was ready, stressful testing regimes, useless indigestible facts, passiveness and a lack of social relevance. Steiner once said there were three effective methods of getting children to learn—fear, ambition and love. He suggested we could do without the first two. But we could also say 'a spirit foreign to life' would be an education cocooned from life, sheltered, introspective, exclusive, elitist and confining itself to social ivory towers, concerned only with its own values (however noble they may be), an education that prefers to admire the landscape rather than work to shape.

Rudolf Steiner intended Waldorf education to be a preparation for life.[1] That means a preparation for being *competent* in the world of work since everyone has to make his/her way in the world of work, in one way or another. This does not mean, however, that education should follow the dictates of the economy, or political ideology for that matter. Education should follow human nature, should orientate itself to the universal nature of the developing human being, whilst addressing the specific needs of individuals in their time and space.

Such an education can help the next generation design and create a society and world of work that itself can support human development. Work is to become more and more an activity that not only embodies the highest potential for individual development but one that serves the needs of humanity and the natural world in a selfless way.

The renewal, one could almost say the *redemption*, of social, economic and spiritual life will depend on the coming generations being able to bring something new, something out of their own inner resources, something that was not there before. What was there before has led to all that is bad in the world (and to what is good, of course). They will only be able to do this if they can develop the potential that sleeps within them. That potential has to become, in its highest form, *spiritual competence*—the ability to do and understand the good, what Rudolf Steiner called *ethical individualism* in his book *A Philosophy of Freedom*.

If the task is to 'become competent in life', the question is: what kind of competence is needed today? Without doubt we can take Steiner's lead in seeing 'the important thing is learning to learn... It is important that we discover an educational method where people can learn how to learn, to go on learning from life their whole life long.'[2]

The Royal Society for the Encouragement of the Arts, Manufacture and Commerce (RSA) in the UK is just one of several respected institutions that have researched the question of the changing world of work and its consequences for education. One of their key findings is to identify the ability to *understand and do* as central to the new competencies. This aptly sums up the essence of Waldorf educational aims: not only to be able to understand but to be able to do as well. We might add: to understand and do out of *insight in freedom*.

Our pupils don't just need to acquire competencies to cope with the demands of a changing world. Society needs them to be able to translate their potential into the ability to regenerate society, to contribute to the resolution of conflicts and to solve the world's problems.

It is perhaps in this realm that Waldorf education has changed since Francis Edmunds' day. Learning through doing has acquired a far greater emphasis. Young children in kindergarten and in the lower school classes need far more movement, including work and play, in order to help them develop their bodily senses and thus acquire the sense of inner equilibrium that underpins calm alertness, the ideal condition for learning. So much in young children's lives has changed that school must now provide much that previously was learned at home or in the streets. Many children today suffer anxiety, nervousness, lack concentration and are often unfocused and dissatisfied. There are many causes of this complex of symptoms, but helping children mature their sense organs, especially those related to bodily awareness (proprioception, balance, touch, sense, movement), is essential to help them feel at home in their bodies.

Furthermore we increasingly encounter an acceleration in bodily growth and development, including the onset of puberty, an early awakening of intellectual abilities and the sense of self. Many practitioners describe children as being more individual in their needs at a much earlier age. We also see a dramatic increase in allergies, psychosomatic conditions such as headaches, stomachaches as well as depression, anxiety and mental illness among children at a time when they should be healthiest. Though Steiner made frequent reference to the link between education and health, it has been the discovery of the medical principle of salutogenesis ('that which makes one healthy') that has highlighted the role of education in establishing not only bodily health but psychological and spiritual health.

Briefly put, health-creating forces are nurtured when children develop a feeling of coherence. This requires a sound bodily development so that the individual feels at one with their own bodily processes, and that they can 'digest' what life feeds them. This means healthy nourishment both for the digestion and for the senses. Sense impressions have to be capable of assimilation because only then can they sustain a sense of coherence between the individual and the world. Coherence is also experienced when we learn things in context. Context creates meaning, makes sense of our experiences. In our highly technological world many processes that surround children are literally incomprehensible; as a result they often lack a sense of reality. When this world is apparently devoid of higher meaning, through the loss of traditional forms of social coherence, the overall sense of meaning and purpose is much harder to find. It is very little use simply telling children that the world has meaning; they have to experience it and to a great extent participate in creating it.

In response to these overall changes many Waldorf kindergartens and schools have introduced a whole new emphasis to their work. The cultivation of fine and gross motor skills, the cultivation of rich, varied primary sense experience, the need to learn how to play and be creative, all become central to the educational task. Kindergarten always had these elements, though now children require more stimulation and examples. They have to be taken out more so they can experience the elements of nature and the weather. They need to experience primary human economic activity, such as food preparation, looking after animals, manual work of all kinds, since these experiences have disappeared from their lives except on television or in books.

The biggest changes are occurring in schools, where moving classrooms are being created, so that the children no longer spend much of their time sitting at desks. Classrooms become flexible spaces, where a range of activities with much movement can be instigated; furniture becomes more flexible. Instead of the school day being fragmented into periods (with bells ringing like alarms), the learning experience is integrated and specialists come and go to offer their foreign languages or eurythmy. The children experience the day as a whole, joined-up, meaningful experience.

These are just some of the many ways in which Waldorf education[3] has changed in its educational provision since Francis Edmunds taught. The principles that he so clearly explains here in this book are as relevant as ever.

Martyn Rawson
Stuttgart, March 2004

INTRODUCTION

What are the distinguishing features of Waldorf education? This cannot be answered, as some might expect, in a nutshell. If one were to attempt to do so, one would have to say it embraces a new view of the whole of life, in particular of the human being in his threefold nature of body, soul and spirit and, therefore, also of the successive phases of childhood leading on to adulthood. That is saying a great deal, and yet might not mean a great deal to a parent seeking answers.

Michael Hall is now over sixty years old. About fifty years ago, when still a young school in Streatham, London, known as the New School, the teachers wondered what impression their work would make on a formal educator. Therefore, they invited a friendly inspection by the Ministry of Education. This led to a visit by several inspectors for several days. In the summing up, the leading inspector, speaking on behalf of himself and his colleagues present, said they were much impressed with what they had seen of the children, their easy yet respectful manner and the quality of their work. Then he added, 'We have seen every type of school in this country, state schools, (British) public schools, progressive schools, various private and denominational schools—the ethics may have been different but the education was essentially the same in all of them. In regard to curriculum questions for this or that aged child, we knew exactly where we were. This is the first school we have encountered in which the philosophy of the school has so far altered the customary curriculum and treatment of subjects that, to find our way, we had each time to ask again.' They did not seem perturbed by this but only interested. At the end they recommended the teachers to wait a while longer until the upper school was better established before applying for formal recognition. It was clear from their manner that they anticipated no particular difficulty.

It was a full twenty years later, after World War II, when Michael Hall, no longer the New School, was newly established in its home in Sussex, that the teachers thought they would again ask for an inspection before they were to be formally inspected by law—a requirement rescinded some years later. The encounter of inspectors and teachers was again one of growing cordiality. The 'recording inspector' paid a preliminary visit to feel the lie of the land, having never before visited a Waldorf school. He was a mature and far-seeing man, much experienced, serious, yet of great geniality. In a conversation during that first visit he expressed the view that what would matter most in the coming inspection would not be to examine in detail what this school did compared with others, but much more to recognize what lived centrally in the school giving it its character and permeating every aspect of it to make a unity of the whole. He could not state in words just what this was, but he had *seen* it and he could only hope his colleagues, when they arrived, would see it too—which most remarkably they did. It can only be described, in retrospect, as a model meeting. It was not that they were lacking in criticisms, or in offering suggestions, yet these came secondary to the overall picture they had arrived at together. Their visit resulted in a unanimous recommendation to the Ministry of Education for recognition of the school both as an efficient primary school and as a secondary school competent to prepare its students for university entrance. Indeed, they had studied the records of former students at college and later in their vocations and found these satisfactory. They were amazed that scientific notebooks could be made so beautiful and asked to take some away with them. The printed ministry report re-echoed all this in very positive terms. The recording inspector said privately at the end: 'You have set up the conditions you need for carrying out your own work, but you are also preparing what should eventually flow into the whole of public education.'

Our challenging times

It was not the object of either group of inspectors to delve into the philosophy underlying Waldorf education. They judged by what they saw and this led them to conclude it was a *good* school, it did good to the children.

With enquiring parents, for whom this book is primarily written, the matter is different. They are about to commit their children to a school about which they may know little or nothing. There are parents who take the school at its face value and, having placed their child, are content to wait and see how things work out. If their child is happy, there is little more they need do about it. Their problem arises when they have to explain to their relatives, friends or neighbours why they chose that unusual school. They may find themselves hard put to it to explain, but they get by it somehow. The others may not be too impressed by their halting, semi-articulate answers—but, who knows, perhaps they too will see it one day!

There are other parents who feel they must understand more before they can come to a responsible decision. They want to know something of the underlying principles, or better, the moral and spiritual grounds on which Steiner education is based.

We hope this little book will help the first type of parents to find the words they need, and that it will provide the second type of parent with the stimulus to pursue the study further, and, in course of time, to be able in turn to help other new parents. Then it will not all be left to the teachers.

To begin with we need to see clearly the conditions of our

time into which children are born, and then to see how this education sets out to meet them. We need to step back and take an impartial look.

We are obliged to recognize that we live in a highly intellectual age, one given over much more to theory than to genuine insight. Such theories and the practices arising from them invade the lives of the young when they are most receptive and least defensive: the younger the child, the deeper the effects.

Our modern, theoretical knowledge does not, in fact, grasp or explain the true being of man. Beneath all that the average human being knows of himself, there live hopes, longings, aspirations, dreams of the might-have-been or the might-yet-be, unused gifts, maybe, that are urging to be realized—all these play into conscious life from inner depths, shaping what we meet as disposition of character. They are real forces welling up from within; left unresolved they lead to the sense of frustration so often to be met both in private and in public life. There are great discontents in the world at different levels, and they make for a sick age.

Witness how in this one century, not yet ended, we have had to face two global wars and all the resultant ills with which we are still contending. See the lapse into dictatorships, great and small; the drift even in the so-called democracies towards centralist controls, to the detriment of free initiatives; the unending conflicts and lesser wars on so many fronts; the ever-present menace of escalation towards unthinkable nuclear disaster. Observe the seething racial and political unrest; the disruption of countless homes, and resulting instability in the victimized young; the increased callousness of crime, including the extremes of juvenile delinquency. Everywhere we live in insecurity in the present and anxiety for the future. Even the brilliant advances in technology accentuate new dangers and bitter rivalries—each new discovery demands an immediate counter-discovery to hold it in check. The younger generations feel trapped in a world which belies all natural idealism—and to cap it all there is the spectral menace of unemployment, paralysing the healthy impulse to be at work and leading to violence born of despair.

Facing all this, we turn our gaze to the tender, new-born infants, in all their innocent dependency on whoever and whatever is to greet them as they enter this world. They have hardly begun to use their eyes and ears when they are subjected to the deadening effects of the unreal sights and sounds of the public media; and before they have begun properly to articulate they are given computer toys to deaden the very beginnings of their original thinking faculties. All these conditions have become a fact of life and we can neither avoid nor annul them. Facing all this we can agree with Hamlet that 'something is rotten in the state of Denmark'.

But where shall we find the villain of the piece—where but in the mind of man himself? There are two psychological demons at work. The one goads man on with extravagant visions of ever vaster accomplishments until he begins to conceive of himself as a kind of god—that is the tempter called, of old, Lucifer. The other entangles man more and more in matter, convincing him that, in fact, he is no more than the dust he is made of—that is the ancient deceiver, the father of lies, Mephistopheles, or Ahriman. He would convince us with Macbeth in his final defeat that life is 'a tale told by an idiot, full of sound and fury, signifying nothing'.

These are the hidden monsters, externalized in public life. How are they to be met and overcome, for the sake of children growing up? How, for their sake, can we build their faith in a world laden with mistrust, their hope where there is so much despair, their charity of heart where there is so much enmity and hate? Are we exaggerating or describing facts? Here are the true tasks before the educator. We may not diminish the enormity of the tasks; we have to grow to meet them.

Once we have recognized the inadequacy of our modern, everyday thinking to grasp the realities of life, above all where they concern the human being most inwardly, how thin and barren it is and lacking in feeling, how shallow in moral content, we may turn with alarm to see what we are really doing to our children. We can see how powerfully and unrelentingly our mechanized and soulless environment works upon them, and how an education which works for superficial results and builds on futile memorizing vitiates more than it aids the hidden potentials of childhood. It is not to be wondered at that we meet with so many negatives in the young: precocious judgement, lack of trust and belief, rejection of authority, mental and moral maladjustment, absenteeism from school, and frequent cases of delinquency and vandalism. These can be seen as protests against life as it is. 'The soul,' says Rudolf Steiner, 'needs nourishment as well as the body.' But what if teachers fail to distinguish stones from bread? That may seem a very harsh statement but the negative facts are universally known and need to be accounted for. An education which fails to feed the deeper forces of childhood represents not only the absence of a good but becomes a source of ill. It undermines rather than builds up hope and promise for a better future. Cleverly conceived programmes we have in plenty. The intentions are good, but the generations of human beings do not grow stronger, and the world situation does not improve.

Some guiding thoughts

Rudolf Steiner (1861–1925) is a phenomenon of our time. Himself trained in mathematics and science, and at the same time having also acquired a wide survey of the humanities and the arts, his main endeavour was to counter the narrow deterministic conceptions which dominate so much of modern outlook and research. He saw and addressed himself to the latent possibilities in man of advancing beyond the present-day accepted limits of cognition to awaken, through self-discipline and exercise, to a knowledge of the spiritual worlds underlying outer existence. That means that man himself properly belongs to those higher worlds. When man applies his will to an outer object, say a spade, he brings about an objective change in regard to the soil. This is a first step towards a productive garden or field. Similarly, if he learns systematically to apply his will to his own thinking as the instrument for knowledge, his thinking eventually undergoes a transformation; he no longer sees himself as the plaything of outer world processes, but his thinking becomes invigorated so that it can penetrate directly to the creative forces at work in the world—it becomes a God-thinking, a creative force itself. Through such thinking man may hope to become the active initiator of his own future instead of drifting, as he mostly does today, upon the tide of events. Rudolf Steiner's method of work calls upon man, in the highest degree, to face and outgrow himself. Then only can he hope to grow beyond the limiting circumstances which hem him in and press down so strongly upon the children.

Rudolf Steiner, by the methods he describes, was able to arrive at quite special powers of insight into human nature. Out of this insight he could then evolve a form of education addressed to the full measure of a human being in his thought, feeling and will. We, too, with his help, may arrive at a totally new conception of man—we may learn to see him as a being of body, soul and spirit, and so bring into practice an education which attends to all three, a knowledge which gives the teacher quite new possibilities of helping children towards a healthy, harmonious and fruitful development of their faculties.

For one thing, we are led to a quite new appreciation of
what we mean by individuality. The single human being not
only fulfils a general law of nature—which might be said of
any species of animal—but is seen to be a particular and
irreplaceable expression of the divinely creative forces which
have brought him into existence. Heredity and environment
produce the necessary physical conditions, as is the case with
the animal, but it is our own spirit alone which can determine
the course our life is to take. This is already present from birth
and gradually lights up in consciousness, beginning with the
first utterance of the word 'I'. Childhood thus acquires a quite
new significance when we can view it as an incarnating process which partly conforms to the laws of physical nature but
partly also transcends these in accordance with higher laws.
We begin to see that the true nature of man lives in his *non-
nature*, in what enables him by degrees to raise himself above
nature, to transform himself and the world around him. That
is the being we serve as educator, but for that we must know
something of the laws that rule in childhood, its state of
dependency on the way to the independent, self-determining
life of the adult. The richer the force of this hidden individuality in the child, the more abounding in quality is the life
that ensues.

Who can account by ordinary methods for a Michael-
angelo, a Shakespeare or a Beethoven? Yet they were all three
little children once and had to discover their faculties in the
course of growing up. So it is in some degree in every human
being. Every child is on a similar voyage of discovery and self-
discovery and we, as adults, can help or hinder. Childhood is
an awakening as well as a growing-up process; it leads from
the 'sleep of infancy' to the 'dream of childhood', to the
'lighting-up of adolescence', to the 'responsible thinking of
the adult'. The spirit we serve as parents and teachers reveals
itself in a physical-material body, but it cannot be *explained*

by the laws of physics or matter. How modern human beings can arrive at a working knowledge of the spirit in terms compatible with a scientific outlook is described by Rudolf Steiner in his teaching of anthroposophy or modern spiritual science; this illuminates the facts of physical-material science from a higher source. This higher source dwells in the human being himself; he has only to reach it.

Childhood is the shaping of the instrument for the life of the adult. In the course of childhood there are revealed, stage by stage, capacities, predispositions, also weaknesses and obstructions. By entering into these with understanding, we may, as educators, help greatly in the process leading to conscious and responsible adulthood. Just as a gardener can help his plants by bettering the conditions in which they grow, so may a teacher, by removing unfavourable influences and promoting conditions harmonious to child nature, help the individuality in each growing child to come to better fruition. Such an intervention is the opposite of any attempt to mould the individual to a given pattern, but the aim is to do everything possible, out of an objective study of nature and human nature, to help each individual to become *more truly himself or herself*.

The object of Rudolf Steiner education is to aid children so that as men and women they may bring their powers, their own innate and sacred human qualities, to greater fulfilment. It is an education which serves *the freedom of the human spirit*. It has been given freely to the world. It is in the world. The distinguishing feature of a Waldorf school lies in the endeavour to practise it.

1
THE FIRST THREE YEARS
OF CHILDHOOD

A moment comes when a mother-to-be knows that a child is on the way. In that moment her life may feel enwrapped by a great mystery. She may recall the Annunciation to Mary in the Gospel of Saint Luke. Since man is made in the image of God, it is surely not impossible to imagine that a like annunciation attends the conception of every human being. A being is about to enter the physical world by way of flesh who is himself not of the flesh. He has to bring with him something into this world but his source of being is not of this world. What, we ask ourselves, is not of this world? Christ said, 'My kingdom is not of this world.' Rudolf Steiner interprets this kingdom as meaning the *I am*. The *I am* in me I cannot find anywhere in the kingdoms of nature around me. Science attempts, in one way or another, to describe the composition or the origin of the body, but it has no access to that centre of consciousness in me out of which I utter the *I am*.

John the Baptist, and later Christ himself, declared, 'The Kingdom of Heaven is at hand.' Rudolf Steiner relates this to the new event coming to mankind with the descent of Christ, the divine *I AM*, to the earth—the entry of the experience of the *I am* into the flow of human history. Until then man was guided by the Law which ruled from outside, for instance in the Ten Commandments, but since the coming of Christ he has learnt to seek the Law within him. It is in this light we may learn to look to the being who from other, from divine sources, seeks to enter this world through the mother. This is not commonly understood today, and therefore one thinks of a human being as derived from and belonging wholly to the physical-material outer world. One does not know how properly to welcome the being that is approaching incarnation, nor do we realize how hurtful this ignorance and misreading of the realities are to that being—what a cold, unwelcoming entry this makes for him,* how the deep loneliness we experience has its origin in this. We may consider, by contrast, the picture of the *Sistine Madonna* and the way she bears this child down from the angel world, and how there are some down below who perceive this. Even if we receive the body of the child with gratitude and caring love, his immortal being from beyond the bounds of birth and death we do not know. But we may learn to carry this in our thought and devotion to the child in our midst. If this thought could find a home on earth, that alone could change the present condition of mankind utterly. Each mother who brings a child into the world can serve the whole of life in serving this truth in relation to her child, for truth is a heavenly seed which multiplies and the world has never had greater need of it in the hard times in which we live and in which your new-born child is to grow up.

And now the child has arrived. There he lies, the most helpless creature in creation, utterly defenceless and depending on how and where he is received, and by whom. Day and night makes no difference. He knows without a timetable when he wants food and knows how to cry until he gets it. Beyond that, he cannot even lift his head which is large, heavy and still, compared with the smallness of the limbs and their vigorous but undirected movements. He gazes past us into endless space or right through us, and to all appearances he could be anybody's baby except that the parents look to see whose features they think they recognize

---

* To avoid the awkwardness of using both forms, we will alternate gender from chapter to chapter.

in that diminutive face. The mother's parental care flows out to the baby, almost too much at times. We know from later experience that even the tiniest babe is longing for love. Children adapt badly in life—we call them maladjusted—if there is a lack of love to greet them and welcome them into life; but also the excessive demonstration of fondness, which can in fact be selfish, can be harmful and the cause of trouble later. Reverence for the little stranger will serve to hold the balance. But without love life cannot prosper, and at no time is this more real than from the beginning.

It is not long before things begin to happen. After about six weeks—times vary with children as they do with adults— there comes the magical moment of that first smile—but almost along with it, or very soon after, the first real tear. That smile and tear are the beginning of human language— confined to human beings alone. Darwin spent much time studying the grimaces in animal physiognomies in search of human origins, being so convinced that man is derived from animal origins—a fascinating study but it led to nothing more conclusive than that animals also have emotions, likes and dislikes, advancing with desires or retreating through fear and antipathy. There is nothing to compare with the warm smile of human recognition or the depressed look or tear at being disregarded or rejected. The smile and the tear are indeed the first rudiments of human intercourse. Laughter and tears, comedy and tragedy, run through the whole of life.

That lifting of the heavy head is the first task allotted to the little limbs, arrived at with much stressing and straining. That, too, is only a beginning. In the months that follow the child will start sitting upright, at first with some support but then unaided. And now it will not be long before the child is off on its exploration as a crawler, reaching out to touch (and even taste) whatever meets him on the way—the mother enjoying the spectacle but with a wary eye.

And then comes the further important stage when, by an inner and irresistible urge, the child is determined to raise himself upright on his own two legs, at first clinging to whatever object, living or otherwise, is there to help, but then standing freely and alone.

It is to be noted that all this progress, generally within the compass—somewhat more or less—of a year, proceeds entirely from inner causes and is in no way promoted from outside, nor should it be.

Whoever has had the good fortune to witness the actual moment when the child stands upright for the first time on his own could scarcely have failed to experience something like a flash of triumph light up in his eye, the first overcoming of the weight of the earth's down-pulling gravitational force. This upright stance, like the smile and the tear, distinguishes man from all other living creatures; and the child achieves this out of the promptings of his own nature, by his own inherent power of will. It gives promise that by the same human will man is destined to achieve his ultimate freedom by overcoming the world—for this will is a spiritual force transcending matter. This potential lives in every child.

It belongs to the blindness of our time that we still perpetuate the idea that man is an animal derived from the animal. People who think that way fail to see how for the little child coming to the upright means that the whole orientation in space becomes different, the child's whole bearing is different, and that quite new faculties are born which can neither be derived from nor attributed in any way to the animal.

To maintain himself in the upright the child also has to acquire balance, and then comes the step forward and the beginning of walking. And thus, by his own efforts alone, he has achieved the mastery of the three dimensions of space.

But then one could carry the matter further. We speak of an upright man, of a man of balanced judgement, of a man of courage who steps forward to embrace something new. Our language declares the deep connection between these first elementary achievements at the dawn of a human life and these high ideals for the whole of life. The physical can be the bearer of the moral. When talking to some professional gymnasts I was able to show them that in training the body they were also helping to build up character. I told them about Bothmer gymnastics as taught in Waldorf schools— that in very truth one can begin to see the body as a temple from which all other temples have originated, bearing witness to the divine.

The great achievement of the first year is to gain control of movement; of the second year, to enter into speech; in the third year, to awaken to the light of thought.

How we speak before a little child is of great importance. He enters into his mother tongue not only with his ears, but the delicate, most sensitive organ of the larynx vibrates with every sound that reaches him. We can say his larynx dances into the sounds we make, refined or coarse, and this stamps something for the whole of life, very difficult to eradicate or alter later. That, too, is why baby talk is injurious; it may amuse the adult but not the child whose profound endeavour it is, albeit unconscious, to arrive at the finest quality of language.

And now, in the course of the third year, a new wonder arises, the birth of the 'I'. Hitherto the child has called himself by the name others have given him—'Tom wants ... Mary likes...' The 'I', to be experienced, has to light up from within. This is the first realization of 'self'. Previously the child was a being carried on a stream of events of which he retains no memory. Now he is *present*, a *personal* memory begins. For the rest of life all memories of the experiences will be gathered round the 'I'. An autobiography has begun. For the parents, too, this event brings a subtle change; they, too, will be remembered from now on. They know their child so very well, and yet, confronting the person coming to expression in the 'I', they can well ask, 'Who is this stranger that has come to join his destiny to ours? What does he ask of us?'—a question that will never be fully answered, in this life at least.

The achievements of the first three years hugely exceed those of any other similar period. We could imagine the child carries aeons of evolutionary time towards us, yet comes with all the helplessness described earlier. The child comes seeking for the loving embrace of the mother, the protective care of the father, and the conditions compatible to his tender needs. He is, as Rudolf Steiner says, wholly a sense organ, absorbing everything the environment offers good and bad into his being, and this goes, very deep, into breath and blood and body metabolism, preconditioning health or illness later. Our modern environment, with its noisy, garish, hurry-skurry, could scarcely be less favourable. The child needs protection from this as far as possible. He needs above all his mother. In her loving presence all is spring and sunshine. In her absence life turns to winter. How many live in a frozen life today?

With the mother there, the child can feel at home. But the years speed by! How long can this close intimacy last? Often, today, the child is placed with a care group before the age of three. Of course, modern life makes many demands on us, but it is better to safeguard the infant for as long as possible from too much change, variety and noisiness, which can leave him feeling lost and insecure.

And yet, life having become what it is, with the mother having to be out working or engaged in other interests, we can be immensely thankful that there is today a widespread movement of Waldorf nurseries and kindergartens where every endeavour is made to care for each individual child, providing beauty and harmony and a wise ordering of events and occupations. Yet the peace and protection of a natural, harmonious home life, at any rate up to the age of five or six, must still be deemed best.

2

THE PRE-SCHOOL YEARS

Nursery—Kindergarten

In a Waldorf school, pre-school really does mean what the word says: no kind of formal schooling begins, no reading, writing, arithmetic or regimentation of any kind. There is an ordered life in the way children are received and engaged in this or that activity, adequate scope for free play, there is song and movement, a gathering for a story, but all this flows along in a natural kind of way, quietly guided by those in charge but without undue emphasis or pressure of any kind. Each child is known and cared for, helped when needed, but nothing is over-accentuated. There is thus a prevailing mood of freedom in the way the children breathe and move.

Ideally all this is an extension of home. The kindergarten should be in a space of its own, with open spaces around, and at least at some remove from the school proper, in no way incorporated in it—a little world apart.

Are nursery and kindergarten synonymous terms or do they mean something different? The distinction is not always clear. Most Waldorf schools take children from the age of four, some from three and a half, and keep them until they are ready for school proper at six plus. This is a long span of developmental time. Experience shows that a child of five was very different when she was four. She has definitely moved on in some way. Up to the age of four or maybe four and a half, the children are still much wrapped up in themselves. Even when they are gathered in a group together, or playing together, there is not as yet a sense of the group. The grown-ups (known by name but not yet called teachers), the other children, and all that is around, still lives for each child as part of herself. And time is always in the present—there is no real sense of time. In a picture book, the cow, the milk-maid with her pail, the ploughman in the distance, the farmer leading his horse, the bird on the tree—all this was yesterday, and is today, and will be tomorrow and all is eternally present. And so it is with all one does. It is a dream-world we inhabit. With the five-year-old and older, it is somewhat different. The children are more wakeful, more venturesome, more for trying things out alone or together. And time, too, begins to count for something; each day is its own in the round of the week and is known and awaited for what it specially brings. It is no longer the picture page that suffices but the story. There is eagerness, even impatience to turn the page to see what follows. They want the story. Each story has a beginning and sequel and an end—each story recounts a piece of destiny—a word they will not know for a long time, and yet there is a subconscious feeling for it which begins to stir. For the child of four, going to school is still far off. At five and approaching six there is already a fore-sense leading towards the great step of entering into the mystery of that other world, the school. This is the step from pre-school, and fortunate are the children who can experi-ence this fully as a clear step in their lives.

All this suggests that there is good reason for having the younger and the older children separate, the younger in what might really be called a nursery, and the others in a kinder-garten, though there would be occasions for bringing them together. In both groups it is essentially *learning through doing*, though for the older ones this could be more accen-tuated, made more challenging, though still far from the head learning of reading, writing and arithmetic. To meet these three before their time is like meeting the three witches in

Macbeth rather than the three benign sister fates, the true guardians upon the way.

When, then, should a child begin actual schooling? We have mentioned six plus, but why then? In England this was always considered the right age for the child to leave the Infant School and enter the Elementary School. A Waldorf teacher might answer the why and the when by saying, 'When the milk teeth begin to come away.' This reference to the teeth causes surprise, but there are three main considerations to justify it.

The first is that the shedding of the milk teeth is not an isolated phenomenon. It marks a process which has been going on from birth: the casting off of the inherited organism and its replacement by one that is penetrated through and through by the forces of the incarnating individuality, the same forces that will eventually shape a unique biography. It is only now, with this replacement, that the child can be said to have acquired what is her *own* body.

The second consideration confirms the first. There are twenty milk teeth. They are general in type, and are surface formed so that they come away easily. The secondary teeth are thirty-two in number and are deeply rooted and permanent. Moreover they are diversified in form and function into incisors, eye teeth (canines), pre-molars and molars. Not only are the teeth themselves differentiated in this way, but the dentist knows that every set of teeth has its own character and has to be treated individually—there can be no mass production in teeth. Thus the change of teeth is a transition from the general to the particular, from the inherited to the individual, as is the case with the body as a whole. Something is achieved that will serve as the basis for a distinct and irreplaceable character.

The third consideration is of immediate importance to the educator, and there we are specially indebted to Rudolf

Steiner. It has long been understood and accepted that, except for the teeth, the whole organism is renewed every seven years. The substance of the body is constantly passing away and being reconstituted, but the form is maintained. Rudolf Steiner makes a distinction between the substance and what he calls the formative forces which first created the form of the body, and all its organs, and then continues to maintain them. What then of the formative forces that shaped the teeth? Can they simply have dispersed and vanished? No, they, too, continue to function but in a more concealed or inward manner—they now work to shape the mind in the young child in a life of pictures which, as she grows older, are translated into thought.

Let us give an example. An adult might say, 'The light's gone out!' A child was once heard to describe the same fact by saying, 'Oh, the light's fallen down.' It contains the same thought but the child still has the *feeling* that something, the light, has really *fallen down*. The child, in this, is recapitulating a fact of history, that of a pictorial thinking which preceded actual thinking. Christ spoke to the multitude in parables. They still had a childlike consciousness which could grasp the truth he was conveying in its picture form. For the disciples he had sometimes to translate the pictures into thoughts. They were more advanced in that they were losing the former capacity of picture consciousness, and were beginning to grasp truths directly as thoughts. If we wish young children really to understand us, we have to go the other way, to translate our thoughts back into pictures. Nursery rhymes have great truths concealed in their pictures. The little child can rejoice in them through their sounds and rhythms. She does not ask for the meaning of 'Humpty Dumpty sat on a wall, Humpty Dumpty had a great fall.' The teacher knows there is an immense world of truth in the pictures, and has to work hard to capture their meaning. The children, in the main, simply live them, and are nourished by them. It is the intellectualized child who asks for confirmation that the pictures are true. The same applies to fairy tales.

The change of teeth brings with it a clear change of consciousness, a new quality of awareness in the children, of themselves, of the teacher, and of one another. This can be seen also in their bearing. They are ready to enter upon the second phase of life, the second seven-year period, to be described in the chapter that follows.

We must ask what we are doing to children when we begin to intellectualize them, for example, by teaching reading before they are ready. In the thirties of this century a Hadow Report was issued based on a government research project. It strongly advocated that children should *not* be taught reading before the age of six; but who attends to this today? Who will recognize that premature educational demands on the child sap the life forces needed for further development later? It is often remarked that many children no longer know how to play. It is as though they age beyond their years so that their spontaneous child fantasy forces have begun to dry up. Then, at the opposite end, in public life, we see how incapable human beings are of coping with the problems that beset them, how unable to heal the ills of modern society—they make compromises, which delay but do not solve. Might we not consider that these conditions have their source in the early years? And what further harm do we do by exposing children to the floods of unassimilable television, and deadening nascent thought faculties with computer games which provide answers in an effortless way. How far do we actually wreck young lives through careless disregard for what childhood actually is and its rightful needs?

There have been noble attempts to counter this. There is the instance of the head of the education department of a large university in America. He set up an experiment which he carried on for several successive years. He selected two groups of children drawn from the same milieu. In the one group the children were taught reading by the usual methods, with its demands at the expense of the slower child. In the other group, the conditions were kept more relaxed; there was a willingness to allow children to come to reading in their own time. There was orderly life in the classroom—but without undue tensions. He found without question that the second group outstripped the first by the age of twelve—allowing, of course, for the individual differences there will always be. The evidence was clearly there, that each child has its own tempo and thrives best when this is allowed for, but there was little evidence that anyone gave this serious attention.

We cite an opposite case. There is a theory current that, since a child's assimilative powers are stronger the younger she is, we lose inestimable learning possibilities by delay. At a large conference of teachers in Canada, one of the guest speakers, a man of public standing, enthusiastically described how a child of his had learnt to read by the age of three. This was looked on as a major achievement and was greeted with loud applause. The next guest speaker called on was a relative stranger. He remarked that the last speaker had confirmed from his own experience that such an achievement was possible. A child *could* be taught to read by the age of three! It seemed to him that this marked only the beginning of a process, the effects of which would continue all through life: for we are not only beings in space, we also live in process of time. It is well known among psychologists that effects produced in early childhood can declare themselves quite late in life. To bring a child to read by the age of three means that we demand of her a considerable degree of mental concentration, therefore of greater wakefulness. We might say we draw her more strongly into her nerve-senses, more strongly than would normally be the case. Another way of expressing this would be to say that we produce a premature ageing process. This runs counter to the liveliness of childhood behaviour and experience—we draw them away from the life of the limbs and into their heads. Might we not be inducing, through premature wakefulness, sclerotic tendencies in body and possibly even in mind for the years to come? This is approximately how the speaker expressed it.

The effect was curious. There was a protracted silence followed eventually by a single clap; then others clapped; then this spread slowly through the assembly. Then, where there had been protracted silence, there was now protracted clapping, a slow and thoughtful clapping, as though people were still assimilating the implications of what they had heard.

It seemed cruel to have spoken in such flat contradiction to the previous speaker. The circumstances offered no alternative. Such questions are too serious for mere controversy. This is an extreme case of a general and widespread tendency today to intellectualize children without counting the costs. By robbing the life of childhood we are stultifying the life of adults. Each person dealing with children must decide whether this is true or not.

We are too easily given to clever theories which claim to be scientific. Education, above all for young children, must spring first and foremost from the heart. Clever heads may and do serve well but only if ruled by wise hearts.

We cannot overstress the importance of the first six or seven years of life for all the years that follow. What occurs in these years preconditions the bodily, mental and moral life, therefore also the degree of stability or instability of character that arises later. It is in these years that the forces that are to shape a biography are working at their deepest level. To that extent the little child is very much at the mercy of her adult environment both in what adults offer of themselves and in what they create around them. It is underestimated how much this is the case, and the younger the infant the more this is the case. It is not sufficiently considered to what degree the moral forces and the life processes are interrelated. A harsh, discordant, loveless or even sceptical environment that views the child as a young animal induces something like a slight freezing in the body-forming process, a prelude to moral and physical weakness in later life; whereas a warm, gentle, loving and harmonious environment releases forces and quickens confidence and courage in life in the years to come. The former breeds antipathy, the latter kindles sympathy, two forces whose interplay conditions much of our life. It is an immense fallacy that little children do not notice. What they absorb unconsciously comes back as judgement when, in the course of the years, it rises up in consciousness. It would be wiser to think that nothing is missed, that everything is absorbed. Thus, too, premature intellectual methods of education, as described earlier, subdue life forces which will be needed for further development, and promote a premature wakefulness which is misjudged as real progress, whereas it is really a foreshortening of life itself. It breeds precocity rather than genuine maturation which must always bide its own time.

The whole trend today is towards over-intellectualization, furthered by the mass media. Do we not see the effects in our large-scale social problems? It has been said that the child is father of the man; but we may add that it needs real children to make real human beings, and that to weaken the forces of childhood is to produce insecure adults. How else should whole populations succumb so easily to dictatorship or centralist rule in one form of another? Why should so many be ready to adopt state-determined moral codes instead of individual morality, state control instead of self-directed will? Yet these trends are everywhere. When the state begins to form people instead of people forming themselves, human beings the world over feel they fall short of themselves in coping with the trials of life. But who traces these conditions back to the years of earliest childhood? Hence it is that Rudolf Steiner so strongly advocated delaying reading and writing rather than hurrying them forward. Yet most parents get worried that their children are not learning fast enough.

A Waldorf nursery class or kindergarten sets out to provide a right environment, right physical conditions, right activities, a right example for imitation.

The imitative faculty of the young child expresses an unconscious attitude of deep devotion to life; this, if unspoiled, finds beautiful expression in children's play. If we were half as devoted and 'serious' in our adult activities as the child is in her play, we should be a different order of people. Child play finds its happiest and most intense experience in the natural imitation of all that grown-ups do, for, after all, the unconscious ideal of the child is to become a fully grown adult—everything in the child strives towards this. Nursery education consists in 'doing' and in all doing it is the life of action and of will that predominates. The objects of play should be as simple as possible so that the child can clothe them with her own natural powers of imagination. A rough and ready doll made of a piece of material or even out of a table napkin calls forth these forces of imagination, for to the little child everything is 'alive'; a 'perfect' doll may seem to satisfy but in the end it cloys—it leaves no room for the imagination and therefore works against the original and spontaneous forces of childhood. These creative, imaginative forces spring from a healthy life of will like flowers from a meadow; they are crippled by 'clever' toys invented by clever adults.

Who could wish for a happier sight than the following? We are sitting in a nursery class, children aged about five. It is their hour for free play.

Along comes a little boy. He has found a broom and is walking along smartly, calling out, 'Sweep! Sweep!' As he comes by, his glance is asking whether you might have a chimney for him to sweep. You have only to indicate where it is. He recognizes it at once and is all ready to serve. Have you ever seen such a sweep!

The children have recently had a puppet show. Some of them bring you the wonders from behind the stage. They show you all the characters and tell you who and what they are. They really *are*! Then come others trailing after and carrying something very dangerous. The look on their faces, the movements as they come, leave no room for doubt. What can it be? The wicked wolf, of course, from Little Red Riding Hood—not a make-believe thing as you might think with its teeth and its red, red tongue. No, it is a wolf, every bit alive in their imagination!

And now something else. Five or six children are busily setting up something—just a few nursery chairs. What can it be? It is a coach! Up goes the driver, sitting in front and above. In come the passengers, sitting behind and below. And now, with a toot and a shout, away they go. How intensely the driver scans the road ahead! How full of purpose are the passengers looking out, silent, equally tense! At what speed they chase through the countryside, passing everything by! And now they are drawing close! And now they have actually arrived! Down comes the driver with a proud swagger. Out jump the passengers. Who is there waiting to meet them? Ah, what greetings, and what rejoicings, all talking copiously and together.

What an adventure! What more is needed? Is not this the great world itself? Play for the little child is not just pastime.

What little child really *feels* little? Play is being grown-up. Play is work. Play is the world itself.

'Play' includes painting, modelling, cooking, sewing, building, making things and a host of entrancing activities; it also includes learning nursery rhymes and action songs in English, French and German, eurythmy (a new art of movement by Rudolf Steiner, not to be confused with eurhythmics), simple fairy tales, little plays, seasonal festivals—in fact, the nursery class or kindergarten is a world of its own, a world of dawning creation where life proceeds at its deepest level. The child should be left undisturbed in this world until nature herself declares the time ripe for change.

Waldorf education teaches us to wait on nature. Nature knows what she is about. Her signs are sure if only we can learn to read them. But we have grown far removed from nature. Instead of holding true to her we are ready to fall for any theory that is plausible, convenient and demands little from us. This is not a 'Back to Nature' call but only a plea that we become more wisely attentive to her. The change of teeth is a radical sign that the child is ready to enter upon a new stage.

What then of the child who begins the change of teeth earlier—does that suggest earlier schooling?

No, it does not. On the contrary, such a child needs all the more protection from undue intellectual influence.

But what if a child is already reading, having picked it up without any help at all?

It is not good to negate a child, but you can regard the matter with a cool eye, and quietly engage the child in some interesting and colourful activities, engaging yourself in the process at times, then she will imitate you and be carried by your enthusiasm for this other activity.

As for the child that is tardy with the change of teeth, it is generally advisable to wait. An analogy may be found with the process of birth itself: the child born prematurely needs added protection, care and warmth; on the other hand, the delayed birth causes no unusual concern unless, of course, it verges on the abnormal.

3
THE CLASS-TEACHER YEARS

The Elementary School

The Elementary School covers the ages six to fourteen, thus forming the bridge from infancy to adolescence. Each new class, as it forms, receives a class teacher who stays with it for the whole eight years (see the next chapter). The founding school in Stuttgart was named The Free Waldorf School to signify that the teachers were to be free of outer authorities in building up the curriculum and in the treatment of subjects. It was also established that children would be allocated their classes according to chronological age.

How a teacher looks at life has a direct effect upon the children. It is basic to the character of a Waldorf School that a clear distinction is made between the nature of man and that of animal to a degree that is not yet customary in the world at large. It is then seen that such terms as infancy, childhood and adolescence leading on to a true adult state pertain only to the human being.

The following two examples drawn from the book *Man and Animal* by H. Poppelbaum will help to clarify this.[1]

In the ape there are already some milk teeth at birth. The moment these are completed, which is within the first two years, second dentition begins. There is thus no room for infancy. In the human being the first milk teeth appear only several months after birth, and second dentition does not begin, normally, before the seventh year when the child has turned six. These are the years of infancy.

In the ape the sex glands are mature by the fifth year, and

functioning begins immediately. In the human being, too, the sex glands are ready by the fifth year, but functioning is delayed by some ten years until puberty has set in. These are the years of childhood proper. But even so, body and the life of soul continue to grow and develop through the adolescent years, and, ideally, the inner life of soul should never stop growing.

It is seen that the animal hurries its physical development to an early end, and there it stops, whereas, by contrast, the human being is subject to a law of restraint—he is held back physically, and thereby an education of soul is made possible leading into realms of inner realization and self-realization from which the animal is simply excluded.

There is no denying that the animal has a soul. It has desires and instincts and a range of emotions so far comparable to those of man that Darwin felt confirmed in his view that man and animal have a common origin, a view that today has become open to question. Instead of viewing man from the aspect of the animal, we may reverse the process and begin to perceive the animal from the aspect of man, which is what Poppelbaum does in his book. The following carries our considerations further.

Animal soul is bound to bodily functioning and set in a given physical environment. With domestic animals the same holds true except that human intervention may have modified the life habits and possibly the environment. With pets, dependence on man may have been carried so far as to become a vital factor for survival; they may pine and even die in the absence of master or mistress, exhibiting every sign of distress in the process. Nevertheless, the association still is in a strict sense 'bodily', concerned with usage and habits, and cannot be compared to the inwardness of human soul-relationships. Human soul experiences can arise through the very fact that in man alone the soul is partly emancipated from the body so that in him a self-sustained life of soul, an inwardizing of experience, becomes possible as the basis for *conscious personal experience*. And in so far as this emancipated life of soul can be objectified, can be freely contemplated and even modified at will, we recognize the penetration of the spirit. In this gradual emancipation and unfolding of an independent life of soul, in the gradual penetration of soul-awareness with ego-consciousness, we have the true meaning of childhood, the true passage from infancy through childhood to adolescence and adult life. In this lies the reason why nature is all-sufficient for the animal but only man can educate man. The animal grows into the outer kingdom of nature; the child needs also to grow into the inner kingdom of the human being.

The years from six or seven to fourteen are quite especially the unique gift of man. We make the gravest mistakes if we regard the child in these years merely as an incomplete version of the adult, and if we imagine that elementary education consists in simplifying adult knowledge, watering it down to a thin sort of gruel, sweetened with make-believe fairy tales and other 'amusing' stories. This some people, and clever people at that, find hard to understand. It is easy to confound imagination with what is merely fanciful. It is equally easy to fall into the error of thinking that truth is only what is strictly rational. Cinderella is a work of imagination and we meet the truth it contains repeatedly in history and in life. Sinbad the Sailor is a clever invention to escape the tyranny of being eternally bound by what is rational. The former nourishes. The latter amuses. Both can serve if we know where they belong but, to know that, we need to discriminate between imagination and fanciful invention. The little child, still very close to his prenatal origin, brings into the world a deeply intuitive knowledge of what is true. Somewhere in his being he knows that truth is only truth if it brings revelation of the spiritual world from which he has come. It is this deep sense for truth which lived in the folk of long ago and which meets us today in folklore, in fairy tales, in the great mythologies and sagas. The pictures these contain give nourishment as a kind of heaven-born milk. The young child needs and longs for that kind of nourishment, not for what is merely fanciful nor for what is prosaically true, but for imaginative pictures which breathe of a higher reality. What is thus nourished through inner pictures will later grow into a faculty for powerful, penetrating thought.

The picture we give the child must be a true picture, a picture born of truth. The picture speaks directly through the feelings to the heart; later the truth of it dawns for the mind. So often today the picture is merely for amusement, and truth is nothing but rationalism simplified for child consumption— no wonder that there is so much barren thinking in the world, thinking that time and again fails to cope with reality. The cause for this takes us back to the education, or rather mis-education of the little child. So much is spent today on 'higher education'. When will it be realized that the highest goal of education is with the little child? Higher education—of the head alone—needs to be based on a long, slow development of all other aspects of the human being.

Truly we need to find the child in ourselves if we are to *know* children. We can impress our errors on them but we cannot evade the consequences—retribution comes in the form of fantasists who cannot find the ground under their feet or of fact-fanatics and iconoclasts who walk the earth staring into an empty universe. The greater danger today lies with the latter, a generation whose thinking is so earthbound that they dismiss all forms of higher perception, including the arts, as unrealistic dreaming. Yet they set up governments and rule people. We have also seen signs of the opposite, a revolt against materialistic rationalism either through drugs or by diving back into various forms of oriental mysticism. The hope for the future lies in bringing new powers of imagination into our Western thinking so that human thought can once again testify to a world of higher realities which permeate our everyday lives. To serve this end is perhaps the highest endeavour of Waldorf education—to lead through education towards the new enlightenment which all the best endeavours of our day, in art, in science, in religion are seeking. This places a great demand upon the teacher to pursue a disciplined path towards a higher grasp of human and natural existence. Unless we as adults can learn to reach up to our children as they descend towards us from worlds before birth, they, as they grow older, will find little or nothing to reach up to in us.

A teacher needs to be an artist, he needs to practise *the art of education.*

In teaching children between the ages of six and fourteen, our lessons will be different, both in content and method, from those given after puberty; the consciousness of the child in these years, the way things impress themselves upon him, the way life takes hold of him, are different; it is a preparatory time which conceals within itself what is to appear later. The flower is connected with its stem but it is not a stem; no more is adolescence, still less adult life, to be confused with what lives in early childhood. The latter must be studied for itself— only then can we hope to prepare rightly for the next stage.

Careful observation will show, as already stated, that the change of teeth brings with it a subtle change of consciousness. The forces of soul which are released at this time appear as thought-forces, but they are not at all the intellectual thought-forces of the adult or even of the adolescent. For the analogy to this in human development as a whole we have to go back to the myths and sagas of ancient times; their powerful pictures and imaginations, so penetrated with feeling, precede the age of thought. They are imbued with super-personal qualities belonging to the whole folk or community. The birth of intellectual thought is a recent event in world history; it dates back no further than the Greeks, the first philosophers, and even to them philosophy was anything but the abstract study it has since become. We need only note that the word they formed to describe their new art of thinking, *philosophia*, means *love of wisdom*—it comprises love and wisdom, the two greatest gifts and virtues of mankind. Even a book like Boethius' *Consolations of Philosophy*, which comes much later, shows us what deeply intimate and moral forces were involved: thought was like sensitive insight into spiritual depths of existence, more akin to poetry than to our present-day thought; it gave *inspired insight* into existence—that is how it was felt. Children of seven, if unspoiled by hasty methods and modern inventions like the cinema, TV and radio, think poetically, they think in imagery; their thinking is at the same time an art of feeling, a feeling-thinking born of the forces of the heart rather than of the head, a soul-thinking where revelation follows utterance as with the poet—it is not at all the analytical, critical head-thinking which comes, and of course should come, later. The years from seven to fourteen span an immense period of transition in the history of human experience. By fourteen the child stands much nearer to the threshold of the modern age, but even then his feeling life powerfully colours all his thinking, as indeed was still the case at the dawn of modern times in the fifteenth and sixteenth centuries—he has not yet reached in his development the purely speculative age, the age of self-detachment in thought.

All through these 'uncritical' years (that is to say, the years before the critical faculty of the intellect is freed), when judgement rests in feeling, touched but unpossessed by thought, the child longs for nothing more than for an authority he can trust with heart and soul. In these years the teacher stands before him not only as a person but as a representative of humanity; the child learns trust in humanity through his trust in a human being. In a Rudolf Steiner School this central position of trust is occupied by the class teacher.

What does this actually mean? It applies quite particularly to the main lesson period with which the day begins (see description later). It is here that the class teacher's role is paramount. He meets his children day by day throughout his years with them, introduces all the main subjects for the year, English, History, Mathematics, the Sciences, and so on, and in the process learns to know his children intimately and to watch over their individual progress. After the main lesson, normally between 9 and 11 a.m. but in some countries earlier, his children are taken over by other teachers, specialists in language, music, eurythmy, handwork and other supporting subjects.

He, in turn, has his special subject(s) to offer to children in other classes than his own, and thus connects up with other teachers and meets with children apart from those of his own class.

Thus every child meets several teachers and every teacher meets several classes, giving rise to a close weaving and working amongst the teachers throughout the school. This provides for the utmost continuity between the children and for the greatest cooperation amongst the teachers.

The class teacher does more than teach subjects. He keeps close contact with the parents and with the school doctor if the school is fortunate enough to have one. He *cares* about his children, cultivates their qualities, guards against weaknesses, notes symptoms of poor health, strives to meet moral and mental difficulties; it is his business not only to instruct but *to bring up*, and he uses his subject matter and directs all his

activities to help a whole human being develop. He steeps all
he has to say in picture and imagination; life is a theme with
many variations which follow one another in gradual descent
from the ancient wonders of the spirit to the material and
technological achievements of today. From year to year he
takes up the main theme again, *the being of man*: in the course
of years from fairy tale and myth through ancient history
down to our times, thus leading also via the prophets and the
Christian mysteries to the promise of new fulfilments. The
picture is the class teacher's medium, not the bare idea, for the
former reaches down into the feeling life, the life of soul.
Where all is contrast and movement, tension and relaxation,
light and darkness, beauty and ugliness, joy and sorrow—
contrasting experiences in epochs of history, in types of
people, in plants and animals, in prose and poetry. This is an
artistic and many-sided experience of the world and of man
that is like a breathing within the soul, making it rich and
strong and well able to support the more conscious struggles
that are yet to come. Language teaching and recitation play
an important part in these years, handicrafts, wood carving,
gardening and especially painting, music and eurythmy—
everything, in short, that can further the life of rhythm in
body and soul.

If *nursery class* education may be described as an education
through 'doing', that of the class teacher period from six to
fourteen becomes an education of the feelings and of the
heart. We need a generation of men and women with a
stronger capacity for feeling, for strong feeling born of rich
soul experience—men and women with greater heart. Then,
too, we shall have educated the social being of man, for our
heart is only our own to the extent that it beats for others. The
social element in us lives deeper than the intellect. One of our
main troubles today is that we have tried to intellectualize our
social problems instead of entering into them with imagin-

ation—and imagination is a feeling force. The intellect divides us into our separate selves but the heart, if rightly educated, reunites us again. Only the heart can make the social bond. True community rests in the free acknowledgment from person to person, so that the individual *grows* in his response to his fellows; differentiation then becomes a moral good. The only legitimate way to community is through understanding, not by acceptance of a common *theory* but by each individual learning to transcend his personal viewpoint in the attempt to understand his neighbour—the modern meaning of 'love thy neighbour as thyself'. Until this is realized we shall not see peace. The education we are describing sets out to try to overcome our primary evil, egotism.

As though in answer to his own question about 'the central thing', the recording inspector, at the end of the second inspection referred to in the introduction, earnestly pronounced the words, 'I think you are fighting evil.' What he meant by 'evil' no one asked him. From conversations with him before, during and after the inspection, I would dare to suggest, as a possible interpretation, any influence that worked against the uniquely moral, creative and spiritually free nature of man. It certainly is the greatest ideal of Waldorf education to work for the full unfolding of the individual human spirit.

The social forces we are trying to foster in these schools are much enhanced by the fact that the community of the class during the eight years with their class teacher remains unbroken. Since our concern is for *all* the forces of childhood, the chronological age, not the mental age, is the determining factor for entry to a class. There are no marks, no obvious awards—there is help and guidance instead, and praise or correction as required. Instead of competition the healthy spirit of emulation is cultivated. Experience has shown that the latter is a far more potent stirrer of the will to achievement, the object no longer being success at all costs but sound results. The class, revolving around the class teacher, is like one being of many members, each complementary to the rest; the achievement of the individual becomes the gift of the community.

There are countless opportunities for practising this. Time and again the teacher can draw attention to the happy use of an image, a phrase, even a word in the composition of this or that child, or a comparable instance in a painting, a drawing, the careful setting out of a page of arithmetic, and so on. There are slow heads and nimble fingers, clever heads and clumsy fingers, much room for mutual learning. We recall the instance of a child very gifted in art and handicrafts but exceptionally slow in arithmetic. She seemed quite incapable of grasping the nature of a fraction. She knew that one was one and that the number four was four, but why should one over four with a line between make a quarter? One morning, in front of the class, trying to understand the teacher, her eyes suddenly opened wide—she had seen it! And instantaneously the whole class burst into cheering. A moment of victory in which *all* participated. Such moments can become lifelong memories, now for one child, now for another.

The question may well be asked: What of the brilliant child, is he not likely to suffer by being held back? May he not feel thwarted and grow impatient and discontented? To this the counter-question may be put: What advantage is it to the brilliant child to be promoted, possibly even exploited and made a prize-show, on account of his brilliance? Brilliant he will be in any case but, divorced from a sufficient degree of humanity, will that be any real advantage to him or a source of true happiness? How many brilliant young people have been known to break down at some point either before or after entering college? How many people are there with brilliant minds who seem cut off from life, with lamed wills? It is often precisely the brilliant child who needs our special care. Brilliance we need, but tempered with wisdom and compassion it is no longer merely brilliance. The mind of man, if it is to be robust and healthy, needs the heart to nourish it. A specialist on retarded children once explained to me her discovery that these children suffered from undernourishment of the brain. By means of diet and various exercises to improve circulation to the brain she achieved notable results. I tried to explain our educational methods with younger children, how colour and imagination quicken sympathy, how sympathy works back on the breathing and the circulation, how our whole endeavour with the young who live essentially in their rhythmic system is to avoid abstract, bloodless thought, but instead to deepen feeling and strengthen the will—how in this way we were trying educationally to help all children and to nourish their senses and their nervous systems as she was trying medically to help her particular children. Out of her long experience she could only heartily agree.

We were taken by surprise when the school inspectors during their visit put the unexpected question: How is it that so few of your children wear glasses as compared with other schools? We could only attribute this to the same fact, that the teaching, by being imaginative and colourful, evokes greater interest and response, and that this works back healthily upon the whole body process, promoting even the health of the sense organs. This explanation left the inspectors silent with wonder and apparently satisfied. A right education embraces the whole organism. Thought may be brilliant and yet brittle and emaciated. The hunger for knowledge is good if it is accompanied by a love for the good, the beautiful and the wise; this needs cultivating and it needs time. We need knowledge that is filled with life and minds that are alive in their thinking.

It is most important for the brilliant child particularly,

while he is still a child, to learn the discipline of waiting for his fellows, helping where he can, and, more important, learning from his slower classmates who frequently have gifts and qualities of patience and perseverance which he may lack. But a Rudolf Steiner education is many-sided, appealing to *all* the faculties; and with the younger child especially it is the *all* that matters far more than exceptional proficiency in one respect. We want rounded, complete and balanced personalities whose special gifts are nourished from a fuller source. The community of the class with its central guide, maintained with all the human differences it comprises through the eight most formative years of school life, provides for this. A deeper, richer life of heart is needed to humanize the intellect. If the teacher is wise and if the teaching is wise, the brilliant child need never be at a loss. There is an abundance of activity to engage him and ample scope to satisfy his needs. Let him add body and character to his brilliance and he will be a better and more full-blooded specialist when his time comes.

There is, however, a broader consideration. Rudolf Steiner discriminates between wakeful children, dreaming children, and children who are relatively in a kind of slumber. For the years we are considering, life at its best should be a happy childhood dream. The transition from the pure imaginative life of the little child to the abstract thought of later years should be a gentle process. The wakeful or over-wakeful child needs to be quietened and harmonized by engaging him in every possible form of artistic and practical activity, by presenting him with every possible example of true endeavour, by winning from him qualities of reverence and respect, calling upon him to acknowledge what has shown itself as noblest, greatest and best in others—by teaching him the hard and patient way. The slumbering child also needs careful watching—he may even *appear* to be retarded. Here the method is not to attack the head, which merely produces headaches, but to train the will through action and repetition. Let him learn little, to begin with, but let him learn it thoroughly, from the crown of his head to the toes of his feet. If it is a case of memorizing something, for example, let him go back and forth on the classroom floor, if only for a few minutes each day, clapping and stamping between each word of the line to be remembered; so, too, with his other learning work. Just as we feel best after a deep sleep, so these 'deep sleepers' may have most to give when, eventually, they do awaken; they may be slumbering geniuses who, just because they have so much to express later, need longest to mature. Or their slumber may be an assumed mode of self-protection from this noisy, clamorous world so that the soul may grow in peace. Such children may be won by good-humoured patience and encouragement.

In short, the class as a small community of varying elements prepares for the great community of life. It is a special privilege to be allowed to grow up in this way and to learn from the earliest years 'to bear with one another'—the original meaning of compassion.

From the teacher's point of view, the passage through the eight years leaves little room for hackneyed routine; he has constantly to be astir. His work is hard, but it becomes his life and his recreation for he re-creates himself through it. The children that leave him are his friends for life and so are their parents.

An understandable question: What if a child should not like his class teacher—is it not protracted misery and torture to have to put up with him for so long? In my experience no such case has ever arisen (but see the next chapter). The answer is not far to seek. From the description given in these pages, it will be seen that this education has as its heart and core the striving to understand man at his deepest level; this lifts the thoughts and feelings above the personal and subjective. The question is always what the child needs and what will best meet those needs for his total development. Where the experience of the single teacher fails, he has the collective experience of all his colleagues whom he meets weekly for this purpose. There is thus no room left for petty likes and dislikes, and if the teacher does not have them it is rare for the children to have them. For the most part parents are amazed at the love and trust of their child in his class teacher. Indeed, the gratitude of parents on behalf of their children has been one of the mainstays of our work, and the main cause of its growth.

A very important aspect of the work in a Rudolf Steiner school is the consideration given not only to the 'how' but to the 'when'. Illuminating articles will be found in *Child and Man*, a joint publication of the Waldorf Schools in Great Britain, the United States and Canada.[2] It is our view that the child, evolving *in time*, recapitulates not only the biological laws of the human race, but in mood, feeling and mode of perception relives the entire history of man; therefore the time for introducing a given subject must be considered as well as the manner of doing so.

Parents of young children are confronted with the fact that reading is delayed in our schools—that we follow the slow procedure of going from movement and gesture to painting, drawing and writing, only finally leading over to actual reading. In this we pursue an evolutionary, historical path. If the teacher of the child of six has taken the trouble to engage his imagination with a story; if then, out of the story he selects a picture, say of a wave, and then the child runs waves, paints and draws waves and eventually comes to a flowing ⌇ and finally to the crystallized hieroglyphic W, he has been led along the path of experience to a conclusion; he has not been forced to a conclusion. The child grows connected in limb and heart and eye with this conclusion; it has become *his* conclusion. This takes longer but it brings inestimable benefit. It is so easy to teach the child the letter directly; he then has to accept it as a symbol foreign to himself, a dogma coming at him from outside, and he will do so; the result, however, is that deep below consciousness, in feeling and in will, the sense of having been impressed upon, the *sense of dogma* lives on and later may appear as a constraint of the mind—a feeling of estrangement from a world which merely confronts him and which he may never hope to penetrate. Writing, which for the Egyptians was still a sacred heavenly script, has become for us a mere convention. To the child taught in the way described, knowledge is something born of a world of imagination, a world of experience beyond the senses and the physical facts and yet accessible—he cannot yet translate this into thoughts, but in the years to come his attitude to life will surely show it. Having been *led* to where he finds himself, he is not likely to feel himself so much a stranger on this earth, and may eventually discover in himself the will and the courage to advance from the known to the unknown, from the 'letters' of the world which he perceives spread out all around him to the spirit. If there was a real way down to physical realities there must also be a real way up to spiritual truths! By guiding the child in accordance with a real past, placing each exercise at the right time, we open for him the possibility of a way into a real future. To many, especially at first sight, this may seem laboured, but others will find it sound psychology. And those who have had the privilege of following such children right through even to the age of eighteen, and have held converse with them at different periods during that time, and have then watched them proceeding into life, will know how much truth lives in such matters, and how such apparently slight beginnings are connected with the weightiest results. The 'how' is here the transition from the picture to the letter; the 'when', the time when the child's natural imagination *begins to turn earthwards.*

A further example. A Goethean principle, which science is coming close to rediscovering and which Rudolf Steiner often emphasized, is that the whole is reflected in each of its parts. Thus the whole development up to twenty-one is reflected in each of the three subdivisions, from birth to the age of seven, from seven to fourteen and from then to the event of coming-of-age. In the middle of these three periods, the imitative stage carries on to about the age of nine; there then follows what my colleague, A.C. Harwood, in his book *The Way of a Child*[3] most happily calls 'the heart of childhood', from about ten to twelve; and finally, from twelve to fourteen, a period which anticipates in many ways the birth of adolescence.

Now the age of nine to ten is a particularly sensitive one in a child's life, marked by a variety of symptoms. It really corresponds to that moment in the first period of life at about the age of three when the child first says 'I' to himself and memory begins. Whereas that first flash of ego-consciousness is a purely intuitive one, now there is a gentle deepening of self-perception in the life of feeling. It is the first dawning of the realization of being 'alone' and separate in the world. With some this accentuation of self may take an assertive, even an aggressive form; with others it may show itself as a feeling of insecurity, of wanting to cling to others—there may even be night-fears. Also the children become more attentive to their surroundings, to the habits and mannerisms of their teachers and parents, for example, who are now seen to be capable of *making mistakes.* Sometimes—mostly where there has been a lack of loving understanding on the part of the adults—there are distressing episodes of stealing, as though the child is trying to compensate for a 'sense of loss' by taking and appropriating things. To meet this moment in child experience Rudolf Steiner made a number of suggestions which serve to illustrate how concrete this education strives to be.

For the story-telling material he called attention to the Old Testament. Beginning with the separation of Adam from his God, we follow, through Noah, Moses, the Patriarchs, and so on, the progressive descent of man into earthly existence. Story after story describes how the individual stands in life to realize and to serve that which is greater than himself—that which is 'of God' in him. The sense of 'self' in man finds support in a 'sense of origin' and a 'sense of mission'. Experience has proved time and again what strength, comfort and encouragement flows to the nine-year-old from this source, how his enthusiasms are engaged, his fears allayed: 'I, too, have a destiny.'

As a companion subject the children are taught about farming, about the farmer—and of course the farmer's wife! The farm is a community of life; it includes the creatures, the plants, the soil itself; it relates to the great cycle of the seasons and leads the gaze from earth to heaven and back again; it comprises so many 'human activities', in the field, in the barn, in the home, at the mill—so many forms of service in which man is seen at his best, as the simple servant and representative of God—the master who serves for the good of all; it reveals man as a being who is *more* than nature and yet who stands fully within nature; one who can *order* life for mutual benefit and blessing.

It was at the end of such a period, in recapitulating the work covered, that a teacher asked his class, 'What is needed if the farmer is to expect a good harvest?' The children thought of everything they could: sun and moon and rain and wind and weather, the farmer (and the farmer's wife to keep him up to it, piped up a girl to a chorus of approval from the other girls) and the farm hands, and the farm equipment, of course, and so on. 'Still not enough,' said the teacher. There was a lengthy pause and then a shy, usually reticent boy at the back of the class put his hand up, 'The droppings of the animals!' The children laughed. How stupid not to have thought of this before! It needed very few words on the part of the teacher to evoke a mood of wonder, even of awe, at this simple, everyday phenomenon. Such is the great household of nature, where each thing has its place, where all things serve, where nothing is ever lost, nothing wasted.

The children were too young for the teacher to comment on the lamentable role which man has come to play in this connection—that was to be reserved till they were older.

At another time in the same year the children are taught about house-building and all the detailed skills involved, and how the house, in all its parts, is an extension of ourselves with our daily human and social needs: the dining room for eating, the kitchen for preparing foods, the bathroom, the lavatory, the library for study, the sitting room for enter-taining, the bedroom for sleep and relaxation, and so on.

Or to touch on quite a different theme, the approach to grammar and syntax. Already in the second class (or grade in America) the children will have been introduced to 'doing' words, 'describing' words, and 'naming' words. Now this can be carried further to the structure of a sentence. Every sentence must have a subject and a predicate which tells us what the subject is doing or where he is. Let the reader join in the exercise with the eight to nine year olds. Let him ask himself, for example, what a stone can do, what a plant can do, what an animal can do, or this or that particular animal, and finally what a human being can do. Let him experience the immense, the almost unlimited expansion of possibilities when it comes to the human being. Then let him imagine what this can mean to a young child, how simply through this exercise the child comes to realize, in his feelings to begin with, but later in his understanding, how man represents a totally new dimension of being, one that ranges far beyond his physical needs and limitations, so that he can never be identified with the animal as is the common practice in our times. Once again, so much depends on when a particular exercise is introduced, at what *time* in a child's life according to the inner needs and conditions of the child at that time. The exercise in question suits so admirably the first delicate moment of self-awareness. Somewhere from the depths of his being there is an answering echo, as yet unexpressed, 'I know what the human being is.'

It is actual observation of the child which must be our guide ever and again. The approach to the twelfth year of life brings new changes which must be carefully prepared for, changes which are precursors of puberty. Development varies, with some manifesting earlier, with others later, yet all children at this time begin to grow a little *out of rhythm*; this can be seen very well, for example, in gymnastics, where their movements tend to become less gracious and carefree and demand more thought and deliberation. As the children become more aware of their bodies they also experience weight and gravity differently—the mechanics of the bones come into play, however gently at first. Only now are they ready to study the mineral world, the kingdom of the lifeless, and to have their first introduction to the science of physics. In the third class they studied man as such, in the fourth class man and the animals, in the fifth class man and the plants, and now at the age of twelve, in the sixth class, man and the stones, and also physics: the eye in relation to colour, to light and darkness, to shadows and elementary perspective; the ear in relation to sound, to noise and tone, the intervals, the mathematics of the monochord; the whole body as sense organ for warmth and cold; the meaning of expansion and contraction, within the soul and outside in nature; also a first acquaintance with the mysterious world of the depths, with magnetism and electricity. Details of this must be sought in the articles to which reference has been made. Here it is the time element we wish to stress. Time is not just a chronological affair—that is time reduced to dead mechanics. In the *process* of time, real things happen; in the time process of child development the most vital things happen. Time here means life, and the teacher must be alive enough to know the right thing to do at the right time. To work 'out of time' is to invite disharmony, but to interpret time in the right way needs the kind of insight into human nature which Rudolf Steiner developed.

At about this time, too, children begin to 'shoot' into their limbs, and eventually comes that awkwardness of limb which is the bane and confusion of the young adolescent. To meet this they are introduced, from about the age of twelve, to wood-carving, demanding as it does quite special and controlled use of the limbs; they learn the use of tools, and how to overcome the resistance of a hard material which has to be shaped exactly according to intention; they learn also to experience the sculpting possibilities inherent in the human hand itself. At the same age, where possible, they begin to have regular gardening lessons, again learning the use of tools, and the handling, this time, of the soil itself. The whole of our social and economic life rests on the soil. What better introduction to becoming a true human being on earth than to learn to know the soil in the round of the seasons—but the time to begin this must be read from the children themselves.

In history they learn about the people who made themselves conquerors of the earth: the Romans who, out of their consolidated strength, sent out their legions north, south, east and west, upon the solid highways which they themselves constructed; but also about those same Romans who established civil law and citizen rights and first made room for the *individual* in society. What more solid piece of flesh can be imagined than that of the Roman in his might? And what strength and what assurance of oneself *within the body* does this not bring to the twelve-year-old! The body is the temple of the spirit. The children must make a healthy entry into their bodies—that is their direct way if they are eventually to find the spirit. Always the balance must be maintained.

These few examples from practical teaching will have to suffice for the purposes of this small introductory book. Before, however, we leave the class teacher in his work and the childhood years which are his special concern, we need to reflect somewhat further on what his full role is, and why, if his work is to be fully effective, he needs to accompany his children for the full life span from the close of infancy to entry into adolescence.

It is the business of any teacher to impart knowledge in the best way he can and to attend to the disciplines connected with learning. If he is truly a teacher he will most certainly feel a deep concern for his children and he will enjoy helping them surmount difficulties both in the work and socially as these arise. Yet in most cases today he has a class of children at a given age and only for one year. He has little or no knowledge of what went before and what is to come after. A Steiner school class teacher, however, has a whole irreplaceable life span of eight years. Through the subjects he teaches he learns to know his children ever more intimately as they progress through the years. His business is to prepare them for a healthy entry into life. By the time they leave him he will have introduced them to the kingdoms of nature, to the stars above and the earth below. Through his history, they will come to understand that life is least of all a haphazard affair, but that there are great interventions, there is meaning and destiny. The study of individual biographies helps greatly towards this. His geography lessons will help demonstrate the interdependence of human beings, more in our present age than ever before, and how economic life, and the basis of mutual service it entails, calls for fraternity amongst human beings. It is such threads he has to draw together into pictures and imaginations that can reach children's feelings and fire their will, preparing for the years to come when they will have to find the guide and teacher in themselves. For much that he teaches, fuller understanding will only dawn later, perhaps many years later when, confronting a particular problem or situation, there will flash through the mind the meaning of something said long ago and long forgotten. Such a flash of recognition, rising up from childhood memories, brings an added joy to life and often new courage to proceed. These are the further goals of the class teacher, indeed of any real teacher, but the class teacher has immensely greater possibilities.

In his daily practice, however, the class teacher also has his more intimate tasks. He is not only a friend and guide. He needs in many respects to be also a therapist. The following, by way of illustration, is near enough to the facts to be taken as a case history.

Evelina came up into the first class (or grade) from the nursery school. She was tall for her age, pale, with a slight drag in her movements as though her body was too heavy for her, and very sensitive in her feelings, over-sensitive in regard to those around her. Her eyes had a questioning look even at that young age. She could smile but rarely laughed outright. She tended to draw back into herself and *felt* left out even when she was not. She could not enter easily into play with others and this made her both sad and resentful. On the other hand she painted beautifully and had a most delicate and lovely sense of colour. Alone with the sheet of paper in front of her and the paints or crayons beside her she could be totally absorbed and happy. Her paintings were always admired by her classmates. They were generous in their praise. This was her closest social medium but it still left her lonely.

Her persistent sense of loneliness, largely self-imposed, led to a curious development. By no means an intellectual child, she was nevertheless way ahead of the other children in learning to read. She became a voracious reader but remained one of the worst spellers. Reading was her way of escape from the world around her. She skimmed the words in her eagerness to get lost in the story, but had no time to *look* at the words and see how they were composed. The more she read, the lonelier she grew, and the lonelier she grew the sadder she became. She came to feel she was a kind of outcast and she wanted to hide away.

The class teacher arrived one morning with a story about a seed. The seed had been blown by the wind from far away. It fell into a deep crevice, cut off from everything around it. It was dark and damp down there and terribly lonesome. The seed was most unhappy and lay there sorrowful and without hope. There was a brief moment in the day, however, which was different from all the rest. During that short while the crevice where it lay was suddenly filled with light and even with warmth. It was the moment when the sun high in the heavens passed by overhead. It was then and then only that something seemed to stir in the seed. Was it a dream of long ago or a vision of some distant time to come? At any rate, now the seed waited and waited each day for that moment to come. It lived for that moment and when it came it reached up as high as it could towards the sun. The seed was no longer a seed but a tiny plantling and, hardly noticing it, it grew just a little bit taller each day. At length came the day when it had grown tall enough to see the world around—to see and to be seen. What wonder that vision brought to our plantling, but the greatest wonder was the surprised and happy greeting of the flowers around. What a greeting they gave the stranger, the like of which they had never seen before!

The story made a strong impression on the class but particularly on Evelina. Neither she nor anyone else suspected why that story had been brought to them. The story was retold by different children on successive mornings. It gave rise to class conversations, to crayoning and to painting, and certainly made a difference. One such story is not enough. Some little time later it was followed by another story, but the emphasis now was upon the attitude of the class. There was once a queen who rejoiced much in the flower gardens around her palace. The time was early spring and there was one bed in particular, a tulip bed, cared for by none other than the head gardener. You know how a tulip grows out of a bulb. As the sun grew stronger, the tulip bulbs began to grow eager and impatient to send up their beautiful tall stems and leaves. And now, as the bulb below grew less bulbous, up above there were forming the tulip buds, and presently the flowers began to appear in all their brilliant colours. The tulips were a gay company as they grew in rings of colours in their circular flower bed. There was one tulip at the very centre which seemed to be the slowest, as if it was hiding something specially precious. All the other tulips were waiting and watching for it to open and wondering what that tulip would really look like. There were red tulips and yellow tulips of many different shades. Whatever would this tulip be? Well, one day, the bud began to open, and what should be there but something very dark, not a very dark red or a very dark blue, but something black. This shocked all the other tulips. A black tulip was something quite monstrous. They felt ashamed, humiliated in fact. They felt that the black tulip ruined their whole flower bed. They wondered what the queen would think when she came along, and they wondered why the head gardener did not take this tulip out right away but instead came every day to look at them all but looked longest of all at the black tulip, shining with its own dark mystery. Well, the day came when the queen and the head gardener were coming straight towards them. They trembled at the thought of the queen's displeasure at this black in their midst. As the queen came closer, they tossed their heads indignantly to show that they well knew the disgrace the head gardener had placed upon them. There was quite a chatter amongst them, a special kind of tulip chatter. And then they grew deadly still and silent.

The queen came right up to their tulip bed and said, 'Oh, gardener, what wonderful tulips you have growing there, the loveliest tulips in the whole of my kingdom. How tall they are, what colours they possess, in reds and yellows and golds and royal purples.' Then the queen's eyes fell on the tulip in the middle. All the tulips shivered, wondering what dreadful thing would happen now. Whoever had heard of a black tulip! The queen bent down to see more clearly and her eyes opened wide. 'Oh, gardener, what have we here? This is the greatest wonder of them all. You must please bring it into the palace for the King to see.' The other tulips were taken completely by surprise. They craned forward to have a really good look before it was taken away. They had never really looked before. And now, as the sun shone brightly down on them, they saw the deepest, deepest possible purple glinting through the festive black. A great silence fell upon them. When that tulip was gone, a sadness descended on them all— they all felt lonelier and could not help feeling ashamed as they looked at one another, ashamed not of the tulip which had gone but of one another.

Again, the children had no notion at all why this story had been told them. Added to the previous story, it had a decisive effect. The world is full of story, but to create a story to meet a given situation comes as a quite special gift and brings its own reward. Such timely remedial stories belong very much to the tasks of the class teacher. It has been said that almost every class has a Cinderella in it and that children can be cruel.

Closer observation has shown that when there is a child suffering from a deep insufficiency of one kind or another it tends to draw on the other children and to sap their energies, and this calls forth an inevitable resistance in self-protection. This needs to be remedied for the sake of all.

In her third school year, Evelina gave striking evidence of such an insufficiency. That is the year for the Bible stories as described previously. It can well be imagined that the story of Joseph would appeal to her particularly, he the dreamer with the coat of many colours, who was different from his brothers, who was specially loved by his father and therefore all the more hated by them so that they cast him out and sold him into slavery. But he was destined to become a mighty overlord, a dispenser of bread. The time came when these same faithless brothers knelt before him, not daring to look up at him. And then they heard him say, 'I am Joseph, your brother whom ye sold into Egypt.' Then they were grieved and were full of fear, but he called them 'brothers' and opened his arms to them.

Thus, in the course of the work, one opportunity followed another, bringing healing with it, and then the source of Evelina's difficulties revealed itself in an unusual fashion. When she was about nine she began to draw, paint, model witches, flying or sitting, with or without a broomstick—with their black cloaks and tall hats and great humps on their backs. The teacher was amazed and so were the children, so was Evelina herself in a kind of way. She had no explanation for it. It just happened again and again with no connection whatsoever with the work of the class. The witch had become her obsession. Children have a genius for projecting out of themselves something troubling them inwardly. What was Evelina trying to cast off? The teacher turned to the doctor and the doctor discovered that the child was exceptionally hollow-chested. Her round-shouldered appearance which gave the impression of her wishing to shut herself off had a visible cause. The ever-recurring hump was a compensatory image for the hollow which was actually there. The doctor helped, the curative eurythmist helped (see section on eurythmy), the kitchen helped, so did the art work in colour (the outgoing red rather than the receding blue), and modelling (the convex rather than the concave form), the Old Testament stories with their tales of courage and endurance in the face of difficult trials and circumstances; every teacher helped in every way he could to fill that hollow space. Evelina grew more balanced in health, in her general demeanour and social bearing, more harmonious and more confident. She was getting rid of her hump. Still a melancholic, from being caught up in sorrow for herself her warm imaginative nature learned to stream out more readily in sympathy for the needs of others. She became much loved in the class.

At the age of twelve something further occurred which was quite unpredictable. This child who loved reading so much was forbidden all access to books, even to the strain of writing things down, for she was threatened with blindness. The patience and the quiet courage with which she faced this ordeal won the further love and admiration of all around her. In the end, with careful treatment, this danger was averted. In later life Evelina became a strong and generous character, a successful artist, and a happy wife and mother.

This narrative is offered as an example—every class teacher will have similar narratives—to show how the timely understanding of a teacher can intervene deeply in the life and destiny of the children in his care, and why it is so important to maintain the continuity of relationship throughout the formative years of childhood. Not only in the methods of teaching, but almost more so in the handling of daily life, do we see the true meaning of authority, authority in the service of the freedom to come.

When the class teacher first sets out on his journey, the eight years stretch like an eternity ahead, but looking back one wonders where they have gone. There are class teachers who have gone through the eight-year period three times, four times, in rare instances even five times. 'Do not think repeating the process means that you will do it better the next time,' says Rudolf Steiner. It will not necessarily be better, it will be different: different children, changing circumstances, a new stage in the teacher's own life—indeed, there is no such thing as repetition, only ever-new creation. We can never merely repeat a life experience.

The years between twelve and fourteen are the most subtly difficult to manage. As the children approach puberty, the intellectual faculty begins to make greater demands, with some children more than with others. There are, in every class, children who are eager, almost too eager, to move on, and others who would wish to cling longer to their childhood. While providing new exercises for the thinking, the imaginative treatment of subjects should not too readily be relinquished. There is always the danger of confusing the pre-adolescent symptoms with actual adolescence. 'Truth' even at fourteen rests more in the vivid *experience* of single events, in the noble sympathies and antipathies of given characters, than in comprehensive ideas and sequences; the children are still immersed in the living content of things; the detached and more or less objective survey comes later.

4

THE EIGHT-YEAR CLASS TEACHER

A Clarification

On first hearing that in a Waldorf School a teacher carries a class right through the elementary school years from age six to fourteen, people often ask: 'What if the child doesn't get on with the teacher? Would that not be a fearful imposition?' The fact is that such a case occurs extremely rarely, and this needs explanation.

It must be clear that the class teacher is normally with her class during main lesson time only, that is for the first two hours of the morning. After that time other teachers take her children in the non-main lesson subjects, languages, music, eurythmy, handicrafts, gymnastics, games and so on, while she teaches other classes during that time. That means that every class teacher must have a special subject of this kind.

This arrangement means that the children are by no means confined to one teacher, that the class teacher has a group of colleagues with whom she can consult at any time, and that she serves similarly in other classes in association with other class teachers. Each class teacher is certainly a central figure for her children and their parents, but the teachers together create a *web* of interrelated gifts and faculties. The class teacher, by teaching in other classes than her own, enters more widely into the life of the school.

The picture of a Waldorf School is thus one of the daily interweaving of human beings with their different abilities and fields of responsibility, all united in the goals they serve, which are to lead every child along a path towards greater fulfilment in life. The teacher himself is always engaged in a learning process to further her work. The whole nature of the work carries it beyond the merely personal and protects it from onesidedness. A child is known to several teachers, and, if a problem arises, the class teacher has the benefit of their several observations and suggestions. If need be, the matter is brought before the whole college of teachers for even wider consideration.

In these circumstances, as already stated, an impasse between a child and the class teacher occurs only very rarely. If it does, it has to be studied thoroughly and a solution found. There have been instances where parents' lack of confidence in the teacher has led to such an impasse. In that case, rather than live in this lack of accord between home and school, it is best for the child to leave. There have also been rare instances where it has seemed best to move a child into an adjacent class; every class has a range of a year within it and there have been borderline cases where the actual connection with the other group of children as well as with their class teacher has proved beneficial. Experience has taught that, almost invariably, a wonderful bond of loving respect grows up between the children in a class and their class teacher which carries forward far into life.

In regard to this question of continuity there are other important considerations. How long, we may ask, does it take an experienced teacher to know thirty children or more— really to *know* them, understand them and be able to enter into their intimate needs? And likewise, how long does it take children to grow so accustomed to the quality of mind, the temperament, the mannerisms of a teacher that they feel happily anchored, understood and secure?' And what can it mean in a child's life to have to make a new adjustment to a different individual every year? What can be the effect on young children of being thus uprooted and transplanted year by year during the most formative years of their life—a different quality of discipline as well as everything else?

And what does it mean to a teacher to be for ever dealing with the same age group, the six-year-olds, the nine-year-olds, and so on, knowing hardly at all what went before and without responsibility for what comes after? Where is the sanity in this, which is accepted as universal practice?

We have seen that a child's life is not only a succession of years—it is a life-developing process, and like all such processes there are nodal points and intervals and crises, that is, times of vital transition which have to be specially known, prepared for, met and carried over. All this is part of a teacher's profoundest service, and how can it be achieved without the kind of continuity with the children in their growing, and with their parents? How, in these turbulent times, can we hope to find people with an inner sense of security, feeling strongly anchored in themselves and in their tasks in life, if they have not experienced that anchorage and security in their growing years? All these are questions to be faced. The benefit and the wisdom of Waldorf practice have found their proof in the lives of many thousands of adults who look back with deep gratitude to their years with their class teacher.

Another question arises, 'Where do you find teachers of the calibre to undertake such an eight-year programme?' They are not found all at once. They have to be continually finding themselves, learning, growing, advancing from stage to stage with the help of others in their own school or in other schools who have more experience. There is no repetition of last year. Every year is a new adventure, a continuous exploration, not easy, but in its effect a life-renewing process—a life of growing and developing, maturing and discovering, in intimate working with one's colleagues, a life of dedicated service to the child becoming adult.

At the end of the eight years what happens to the teacher then? He or she should have a sabbatical. Rudolf Steiner's advice was to engage during that year in a quite different type of activity, to travel, to make new connections. Then, if they come back to take a second class through, will that be easier? Maybe in some ways, but it will never be the same; it is not just a case of different children, but children have become different, and the teacher is different, is older and working out of other forces, and life, too, has become different. It will be a new adventure all over again.

5
ABOUT TEMPERAMENTS

A striking innovation on the part of Rudolf Steiner in the sphere of education, but also in life in general, is his introduction of the study of the four temperaments. In the days of Shakespeare and Ben Jonson these were spoken of as the 'humors' or 'humours', related to the word 'humid', moist. They were based on what were regarded as the vital fluids:

blood—sanguine (a sanguine or flighty temperament)
black bile—choleric (easily galled, angered, irritated)
yellow bile—melancholic (liverish, peevish, jaundiced)
and phlegm—as the word suggests, phlegmatic, sluggish

Once we begin to pay attention to them, the temperaments convey much for daily observation. We all must be related to all four, since we all possess the four vital fluids, yet it is striking to note how each of us has a dominant temperament and must take care not to be at the mercy of it. Let us say we all, at times, have a choleric burst of temper—the moment passes but the habitual temperament remains: the choleric is apt to be the most stormy, and later the first one to regret it; the sanguine, feeling she has been caught out, will try to pass things off with a laugh; the melancholic is likely to brood longest and remain in sombre mood; the phlegmatic may be quite startled with herself, then shrug her shoulders and quietly move on.

The temperaments have their virtues and their vices. The choleric is courageous, the first to mount the battlements, but she can also be foolhardy and unrestrained in her ire. The sanguine is generally a good mixer, a good one to have in any company, but she can be easily forgetful, inconsequent and therefore not wholly reliable. The melancholic is thoughtful by nature and ready to reach out to others in their distress— but she can be too busy dabbing her own eyes and is then a general wet blanket. The phlegmatic can at times present herself as a solid rampart of defence if she is not, on the contrary, slowing up all the traffic in the highway. The ideal for us all is to achieve mastery of our temperament, but that means reaching a source in ourselves which carries beyond the play of temperament so that one learns to live equably with all around.

We now turn to the question of how this relates to the education of children. How far is it possible to help children develop the virtues of their temperaments, avert or overcome their vices, and so grow towards becoming 'masters of all weathers' both in public and in private life? We offer the following small-scale incident by way of illustration.

There was once a summer camp in the west of England for children from the Michael Hall School. Quite a contingent, on this occasion, came over from the Waldorf school in Stuttgart to join them so that, together with two or three teachers and other helpers, we were a company of around seventy.

We started off in very good cheer, but then the weather turned out to be relentlessly foul. If it didn't blow it rained and often both at once and almost incessantly—quite the worst it could be. We cooked over a trench fire mostly in rain. We huddled together in the main tent at meal times and for a social hour in draught and in damp. One early morning saw half of the campers struggling out of the tents that had collapsed on them as a result of the wind and on to the sodden ground outside. Another morning at 4 a.m. a brave young crew set out with frying pans and sausages and other delicate viands to march to a distant hill from which to view the rising sun and feast in its honour. They reached the hill top well on time, but then came the clouds, and never a glint of sun; having waited hopefully for a time, they took to frying their sausages while the rain sizzled on to the frying pans, ate hurriedly and beat a hasty retreat, if not for 'home', then at least for home base. Then, half way back, the sun decided to come out in radiant smiles, a poor consolation but not to be despised; and so they arrived in camp, not beating drums or even frying pans, but carrying their heads high—for, after all, they *had* got up at 4 a.m., and what had the others done? Indeed, there *were* bursts of sunshine from time to time, which meant a rush to air the tents and get things dried out.

Yet, with it all, so strong was the resolve, by common consent, and at all costs, 'to brave the weather', that no more than one or two in the whole camp succumbed to a catarrh. The cholerics, true to type, blew their chests in defiance of those dismal weather-gods; the sanguines rollicked with good humoured laughter; the melancholics, looking around and seeing there was no help for it, dried their eyes, buried their handkerchiefs and grew unusually cheerful; and the phlegmatics allowed themselves to be rolled out of their security coverings to do their share of the chores, and whatever else, with unremitting grace. All were happy with all and took pride in all. It was declared in the end with hearty bravado and three loud cheers that this was the best camp that ever was—no one dared to suggest that ever could be. The camp was able to throw a concert to the village in the village hall: music, songs and scenes from *A Midsummer Night's Dream*, with the local MP as guest of honour. He, seeing the British and the Germans so heartily united, made a redoubtable speech about how such a camp showed the way towards universal harmony and peace.

What is the point of this story? We certainly had mastered

the circumstances by appealing to something more than temperaments, yet in a way that allowed each temperament to play its role. In life, too, there are all kinds of inclement weathers. Another of Shakespeare's comedies ends with the Clown, left alone on the stage when all the rest of the company have gone, singing a song, a sad and lonesome song, with the refrain 'For the rain it raineth every day.' Why should it rest with the Clown, dressed in Fool's motley, to be the one to see most clearly the foolishness, the folly of this world? And every young person must go through such a moment of loneliness, of wondering at the folly of the world—far greater folly today than in Shakespeare's time. And then how many take their guise from their temperaments, the rebellious choleric, the careless sanguine, the repining melancholic, the indifferent phlegmatic.

Once entered upon seriously, work with the temperaments, as introduced by Rudolf Steiner, opens up real possibilities of helping children towards coming level with themselves and therefore with the world. It offers opportunities in a great variety of ways, for example in the approach to the four rules in arithmetic, to the choice of a personal instrument in music, to exercise in colour, in drawing, to the distribution of parts in a play preferably written by the teacher for her class, to the tasks she might set for one child or another both in their school work and their services to the class. The temperaments also relate to matters of discipline, health, even of diet, in consultation with the parents.

Rudolf Steiner recommended that children should be grouped in class according to their temperaments. This way the teacher has a clearer command of the whole situation of the class. Her golden rule is never to go *against* the temperament of a child but always to go *with* it. In telling a story, or narrating a piece of history, the teacher should keep the temperaments in mind. For example, should she be describing a monarch, a captain, a situation depending on someone's daring or courage, she will turn quite naturally to the cholerics. She herself will impersonate by her manner and delivery the strength and resolve of the character in question, and her young cholerics will hardly be able to *hold* their seats. If his story tells of a hunt or a chase or a pursuit of some kind, she will, with an eye to her sanguines, develop such a rapid change of scene or multitude of happenings that she out-sanguines for sanguines, so that they are glad for a time to 'rest in peace'. For the melancholics she will select matters of great detail, appeal to their marked thoughtfulness and their long memories, and at the same time miss no opportunity to lead them to forget themselves in entering into the griefs and trials of another. With the phlegmatics the approach is always more difficult.[1] A very effective method is to select a high point in the story when all are agog to go on, and then stop dead, silent, before them; in the sudden hush they may begin to look up with a wondering eye, disturbed for a moment out of their seeming somnolence, and then the teacher must reach into them with force to impress, in that moment, all she can upon their minds. Of course, these are mere hints at possibilities which offer endless variations. Though the children are in groups they are also individuals all the time, and the class teacher must know each one well. She is rather like the conductor of an orchestra, now turning to one group, and then immediately to another, and then again signalling to the one or the other child within a group. Such lessons have to be well prepared, with each child in mind. The whole class is kept alive and moving. Then when the stories or descriptions are retold on the next day, as they mostly are, she will know whom best to call on for one episode or the other.

The grouping of the children according to temperament is not easy. It requires very careful observation of each child, not only general behaviour patterns but in the qualities of the work she produces. Sometimes a teacher will need the help of her colleagues to clarify her own picture. There is rarely or perhaps one could say never a pure single-temperament child. There may be a choleric-sanguine and that is not the same as a sanguine-choleric. There may even be a choleric-melancholic, or a melancholic concealing a choleric. Strangely enough there can also be a type of sanguine-phlegmatic, or a mixture of melancholic and phlegmatic.

Then, to make the matter more complicated, there is frequent evidence of an induced temperament. For example, in the case of broken homes the effect on a child might well be to induce a feeling of loss and abandonment and consequently of melancholy, though the child may not actually be a melancholic. Or it may bring about a feeling of resentment, an inner mood of rebellion against circumstances, and this may induce irritability and anger in a child who is not by nature a choleric. Another child may, in self-defence, build up an attitude of indifference—become a pseudo-phlegmatic. We need to become very sensitive to such matters.

To take another instance: the effect of television. The flood of impressions undoubtedly tends to produce sanguinity and lack of concentration, whilst the physical situation of being 'glued' to the screen can result in a state of inner fixation akin in character to the phlegmatic.

The method of work described here applies more directly to younger children. As we approach the secondary school years the method may still be there though in a more subtle manner. An actual change of temperament is often to be perceived in the passage 'from childhood to youth', that is, at the approach of adolescence. The reader may ask herself whether she recalls such a change in herself. And there are still other factors in an overall study of the subject.

Still to be considered with regard to the grouping of temperaments is the effect the children have on one another: the cholerics in a bunch, all equally ready to leap to the charge, might bring a somewhat sobering effect on each other— choler balancing out choler. So too, several shifting changeable sanguines together, darting in mind from point to point (and in body too, if they could) might have a subduing effect on one another. And the melancholics together produce a curious effect—they cannot compete in weeping as the cholerics can in shouting or the sanguines in darting about; to be a weeper amongst weepers begins to become rather droll. The phlegmatics, each one so enclosed in himself, become uneasy in sensing themselves surrounded by so many silent blocks.

Altogether, the subject of temperaments, as we have shown, is a very serious one. Each temperament brought to an extreme results in its own type of mental illness, such as mania or depression. This shows further how deep-rooted the temperaments are in human nature. And yet, in ordinary life, there is much room for humour, and the teacher certainly must conduct the matter with a light heart and a twinkling eye.

For a delightful description of children and their temperaments we warmly recommend *Childhood*[2] by Caroline von Heydebrand, a leading pioneer of the first Waldorf School in Stuttgart.

6
ADOLESCENCE

With puberty we enter the third period of childhood. It may be compared in history to the passage from the Middle Ages into modern times—an entry into a totally new relationship with the world. Once again soul forces are released which were previously at work within the organism, this time more particularly from the rhythmic system; there is a further readjustment between body, soul and spirit. The forces which are now freed provide the basis for a personal life of feeling; for the first time life becomes a personal affair, an individual questioning of existence in all things big and small. It is not that younger children do not question and that the answers they receive do not directly concern them, but now the emphasis is more on thought. Subject confronts object far more sharply—the need to *justify* relationships, not merely to accept them, asserts itself. The wish arises to make one's life one's own.

This awakening to the inner self first expresses itself as the beginnings of an independent life of thought; it becomes a search through the idea for the 'ideal'—a longing, as Rudolf Steiner says, to discover that the world is based on truth. This longing for the ideal may take different forms: it may appear as a restlessness to leave school, enter life and become an adult quickly; it may be charged with romantic imaginings— 'castles in the air'; it may be seized by vain ambitions or be driven by desires. Much will depend on background conditions and the education that went before. What thus awakens is, at its best, an inner dream of higher goals and possibilities. In the new questioning about life and in the personal search for truth which begins at this third stage of child development, we may recognize the first stirring of the spirit within the wakening human mind.

In a real sense the adolescent begins to discover himself in the world of ideas. He *enjoys* ideas as the younger child enjoys pictures and the still younger child play. To begin with it is almost like a new game—the will to argue, to assert or to contradict opinions—but it is far more than that; this new life in self-sustained ideas is like stepping into a realm of freedom where the inner life first begins to experience its independent nature. Hence the demand for independence which, to the young adolescent, intoxicated with this sweet and liberating sense of freedom, seems so justified, and to the adult, who still views him as a child, so perplexing.

The adolescent begins to question all things: himself, the world, the authority of parents and teachers, the meaning of destiny, the values of life or the value of life itself. It is a moment of release; yet it brings with it added loneliness. The following poem[1] by A.E. expresses this well.

AWAKENING
The lights shone down the street
In the long blue close of day:
A boy's heart beat sweet, sweet,
As it flowered in its dreamy clay.

Beyond the dazzling throng
And above the towers of men
The stars made him long, long,
To return to their light again.

They lit the wondrous years
And his heart within was gay;
But a life of tears, tears,
He had won for himself that day.

It may be objected that not all young people are poets and feel these things so strongly. It would be truer to say they do not all feel as clearly. Among young adolescents, however different they may be, there is still a common bond which is very strong; they will rise up in ready protest and indignation if this delicate sense of self, the birth of the 'subject' within the mind, is in any way slighted or ignored. Puberty means for all of them the end of naive childhood and the beginning of a life of personal endeavours, hopes, loves, problems, sorrows and discontents which they now know they must eventually resolve themselves. They are glad and thankful for a lead from one whom their hearts can accept, and they love the person who can bring them the seriousness they need and yet the relief of golden laughter.

A great help with discipline at this time is the art of gentle and unprovocative humour; sarcasm, for example, can be most hurtful and destructive. In adolescence, life becomes at one and the same time universal and markedly personal; the newly awakened 'ideal' element which wishes to discover truth in all the world finds itself bound and hampered, and the impulse of love for all things confused and fettered by desire. It is not for nothing that Milton, as a young man, wrote both *L'Allegro* and *Il Penseroso*; youth is both gay and melancholy. How can education help? The following description of painting in our schools and the transition to black and white shaded drawing will be one indication.

From the nursery class on there is a weekly painting lesson in watercolours. In the nursery class little more is done than to help the children keep their colours bright and clean and flowing. The colours are dissolved, and they paint with large square brushes on a moistened surface. From the first class onwards, the attempt is made to lead them into an experience of the specific qualities and inherent possibilities of the colours themselves. Just as the letters of the alphabet, limited in number, can build up words of innumerable meanings, so the colours, too, few as they are, may in their interplay express infinite shades, qualities and moods. Colour studied in this way becomes a direct language of the soul. There is much stress laid today on self-expression; but there must be a conscious command of the self, a studied medium, something to express, and the required disciplines with which to express it—that alone is art. If children are left only to do as they will, what benefit can it be to them? Sooner or later it leads to a kind of exhaustion. Gifted children will always produce something interesting—for a time! Then they either fall into habits and mannerisms or grow empty. One gains the impression, at times, that with the self-expression enthusiasts anything 'odd' is accounted remarkable. There are many 'odd' corners in the human soul and the results are sometimes quite 'remarkable'. The only way to real freedom of expression is through careful schooling; this applies to art at all times and to children quite especially. A methodical training in the unique language qualities of the different colours; how they merge and interpenetrate to give *known* effects; how yellow of itself is radiant and expansive though it can densify to resting gold; how blue lends form, how it can hold and also lead into depth; how red can be power at rest, can mount to triumph or turn to anger; how colours can be warm or cold; how each colour has its range and yet how their effects can multiply like situations on a stage between the actors—such a study, through exercise, usage, long experience and discovery, gives the ground for freedom where self-expression finds a legitimate and positive outlet. Children need schooling in all things; and then, in the measure that they are schooled and given the right materials with which to work, their originality will gather force and find increasing range of expression. The colours on the page become moods and qualities in action, and the forms are not 'drawn in' but arise through the play of surfaces and the meeting of tone perspectives. This the young child learns through guidance and experience. The intention of the work is not to produce artists—artists will be artists anyway—but to train a generation of people disciplined through art, to quicken and educate the creative impulse in all children and, in the end, to carry youthful athleticism of soul into old age. If the poet has a young heart why should not all people have younger hearts? This is the mission of all the arts practised in our schools, each with its special skills and opportunities for training. There are people who still think that art is effeminate, especially for boys. Art is more powerful in life than concrete arches and steel bridges! Art carries life along. The soul expands through it to new dimensions.

At puberty the children cease to work with colour for a time and, instead, turn to black and white. This is a medium of sharp contrasts, well suited to the inner struggle of light and darkness, of personal conflict and resolve, into which they are now entering. The pictures they produce are eloquent of this. They vary very much with different children and yet have very much in common. One such picture may be of a dark, cloud-swept sky with a strong shaft of light breaking through; another of a storm-tossed ship with the haven of rest far ahead; yet another of a desolate landscape and in the background a hill with a cross or a chapel upon it; or perhaps just a solitary figure gazing pensively at nature or communing silently with itself. Frequently there is a human figure attacked by daemonic shapes of every kind, as in medieval pictures of the Temptation of St Anthony, and, somewhere above or behind, a being like a guardian angel. These pictures reflect the inner mood; the particular subject chosen is only incidental to the mood. Results can be startlingly unexpected. Sometimes the same child will work through pictures of torment and horror and then, ultimately, reach something tender and sublime. After a year or two, when greater stability has been acquired, there is a return to colour, but to a more conscious use of it and, through the work in black and white, to a clearer appreciation of form.

In the matter of puberty our age is prone to exaggerate the part played by sex. To ignore it is foolish but to regard it, as many do, as the primary and determining factor in life is a gross error. It is not sufficiently observed how closely the *erotic* is allied to the *neurotic*: both are the consequences of over-intellectualism in the sphere of thought on the one hand and undernourishment of feeling on the other. The very fact that there is so much emphasis on 'sex' is itself evidence of the over-intellectualism which this education is trying to combat; soul-starvation is interpreted as sex-starvation.

The impulse of love is an all-embracing one—it includes the whole of existence; the impulse of love for all things also hallows the love for the particular. No one has expressed this more beautifully than Soloviev in his book *The Meaning of Love*.[2] 'The meaning of human love, speaking generally, is the *justification and deliverance of individuality through the sacrifice of egoism*. On this general foundation we can also solve our particular problems to explain the meaning of sex-love.' It is our materialistic view of nature that makes the human soul a stranger in this world and flings people back emotionally upon themselves and their desires; it is this with all its consequences that defeats the impulse of true love and reduces it to a sex episode. Where the spirit is awake and aware, sex is the detail and love the reality. The young adolescent in his newly discovered loneliness longs to find a world that is worthy of his love. He has the impulse to know life and to find in life the ideals he seeks. The following poem in translation is not written by a youth but by a modern poet, Iqbal.

LONELINESS

To the sea-shore I went and said to a restless wave,
'Thou art always in quest of something. What ails thee?
There are a thousand bright pearls in thy bosom,
But hast thou a heart like mine in thy breast?'
It merely trembled, sped away from the shore, and said
     nothing.
I betook myself to the presence of God, passing beyond
     the sun and the moon, and said:
'In the world not a single particle knows me,
The world has no heart, and this earthy being of mine is
     all heart.
The garden is charming, but is not worthy of my song.'
A smile came to his lips, and he said nothing.[3]

Young human beings long to find that the world has a
heart. How easy it is today to give up the quest as foolish.

The adolescent wants to discover the true hero in man, the
fighter for the ideals of the human race, for truth, beauty,
goodness. There is no age without its heroes; they are not
made less because the world rejects them or receives them
tardily. How many prophets have been ridiculed and perse-
cuted here on this earth? The teacher who is himself filled with
the quest for the true foundations of human existence, who
sees clearly how, in our essential being, we contradict and
transcend all natural law, how we are called upon perpetually
to war against the beast which would rob us of our humanity,
how easy is the fall, how hard the ascent, how much, how very
much depends upon us keeping faith with ourselves—such a
teacher will not be lacking in material to inspire and give
heart to his pupils. The heroic calls to the heroic, and to learn
to behold the hero in the human being is to waken the
slumbering forces of heroism in human nature.

All external nature follows given laws; we alone live by the law we set ourselves. Nature reproduces itself but man is constantly producing the new and the unpredictable—he is the great enigma of our modern science because what he truly is escapes all outer scrutiny. The lion is a lion by virtue of its species; the more perfectly it embodies its species, the more perfect it is as a lion, and the same is true of all creatures and of all the kingdoms except the human kingdom. The ideal of the perfect human being, however, is that he shall be the prototype of himself alone. Try as we will we cannot specify the individual—our interest in him is roused to the extent that everything which is more general in his nature falls away; it is not man the species, but the uniqueness of each single individual which reveals to us the true nature of the human being. The creature lives solely by instinct, but man ascends to free initiative, and this initiative, springing from the hidden sources of his spirit, adds ever new content to the sum total of existence. Man has lived through countless hours of darkness, treachery, disruption—through countless denials of himself and his Creator—yet the hero in man adds wonder upon wonder as revelation of the spirit. Egypt is a wonder. Greece is a wonder. Renaissance art is a wonder. These last centuries have produced many wonders. Beethoven's *Ninth Symphony* is a wonder. So is the George Washington Bridge a wonder in its own degree, where complexity has been so far resolved that the law of its construction stands revealed in all its simple grandeur. We measure life by what is creative in it, and as teachers we have the mission so to educate that the creative in us may find utterance; it may speak to us in many tongues and in many modes and still remains the language of man. Today we may point to many horrors which twist and distort the human countenance out of recognition, yet somewhere beneath the vileness we may still glimpse, disconsolate, beseeching, the face of humanity. As teachers we have to lead the vessel in our charge safely through the Scylla and

Charybdis of modern times, egotism in material things and scepticism in spiritual things; the one makes too much of the earth, the other too little of heaven.

The passage to truth, the passage through the Scylla and Charybdis of today, is indeed a perilous one. The one temptation is to regard the human being as no more than a thing in a meaningless world; the other, to convince him that he is a nothingness in himself. In broad and in large these are conclusions the world has arrived at, and it is with these that the teacher is expected to meet the youthful idealism and eager expectation of his adolescent pupils as they press on to prepare for their part in life.

How has this come about? For too long mankind has regarded itself as a detached spectator of the world of nature, quite forgetting that our own thoughts, perceptions, feelings, impulses and actions are not only an intrinsic but the most significant part of the world process in which we find ourselves. We have failed to recognize that our knowledge of the world can only be commensurate with our knowledge of ourselves which, today, is approximately nil. What we know of ourselves is the mechanism of our organism; however we analyse this organism, it brings us no nearer to our true self. What we know of the world is its mass-energy composition in meaningless and never-ending motion; try as we will, we can never come to terms with ourselves in such a world.

What has been achieved in this scientific age no one will deny. It is what has not been achieved which concerns us here. What has not been achieved is to arrive at a concept of the human being by which we can live. From a strictly scientific point of view, however complicated a thing a person may be, he is nevertheless a thing, and a thing can have no claim to being a *self*, far less a self-determining self. Beyond the concept of 'thing' some might prefer the term 'energy-complex'.

If man should imagine himself more than a thing or an energy-complex, he lives in illusion.

This is the point of combat. Such concepts may serve for robots but not for human beings. They give the lie to all claims for higher truth and make life an absurdity. We demand faith from the young and in the same breath deprive them of the faith they have; we present ideals to them and nullify the ideals we present; we pose as responsible people who know the world and daily exhibit our irresponsibility. This, as seen through the eyes of youth, is devastating. Here lies the danger for the young: they must either accept our thesis that life has wants, desires, prospects of a sort but no meaning or they must reject us and our thesis to seek their own unguided course.

Facts remain facts and contain the truths we seek. The theories people construct about the facts depend on how they see them. If they see only their material aspect, then they evolve materialistic theories. The application of these theories leads to results of a certain kind. If they saw differently, they would think differently, interpret differently and arrive at different kinds of results. All depends, in the first place, on the seeing. Rudolf Steiner beheld the same facts but saw them differently. His seeing led him to a spiritual view of the universe and man. Within the phenomena of nature he beheld a higher nature; within human being, a higher human being. He saw, and he taught others to see, that morality is a fact which has its roots in a spiritual world but blossoms through man in this one. Through the human being, also, earthly events acquire eternal meaning. He made the greatest ideal of Waldorf education that young people going through the schools and entering life might, in course of time, themselves arrive at a worthy concept of man, one that would ennoble life instead of debasing it. This is the striving of the teachers also. It is not possible in so short a space to do more than hint broadly at the mood and character of the teaching in a Rudolf Steiner high school or upper school. The work is as rigorous as elsewhere but phenomena are presented and viewed differently. It is the human being who occupies the central place in everything taught. In contrast to the cold analysis of facts as commonly presented, there is live attention to the constructive forces of human thought, feeling and imagination. The interpretive power of the heart is added to the analytical nature of the mind. This leads to the view that the world is a work of art and not a machine. It leads to the view that man is a synthesis of world creation: in him the physical and the moral, the natural and the divine meet. Through his achievements creation advances further.

To take the adolescent through the history and development of art as the revelation of evolving humanity; to educate him into the meaning and appreciation of poetry as the medium wherein the centre in us finds kinship with the heart of all creation; to unfold the nature of love, by way of the great sagas and literatures of the human race, as the human being's search for his own kingdom; to show that the ideals man carries are the pledge he has of his true estate, that there is conception in the spirit as well as in the body, that moral imagination is not a chimera of the mind but a power for renewing life; to discover that history follows a mighty plan of promise and fulfilment, that it leads from a state of moral and spiritual dependence towards the goal of self-mastery and self-determination, from community by blood-ties in the past to community by assent; to demonstrate that nature has depth as well as surface and that as man grows in insight so will the ultimate goal of science be attained, the rediscovery of the divine; to come to an understanding of the spiritual heritage of the East and to an appreciation of the spiritual promise of the West; to see that human beings are made different in order that they may grow more greatly united; to perceive mankind, with Paul, as many-membered, but One Body filled with One Spirit; to learn to see warmly and to think humanely; to recognize the meaning of 'to die in order to live' and to see the many deaths that man must die to gain his immortality; to educate youth to be positive towards others, resolute in oneself, careful in study, thoughtful in observation and self-expression, to pursue all this with enthusiasm and with faith in the attributes and striving qualities of man—to do this is to ennoble the mind, to fire the imagination, to fortify the will and to quicken initiative for life. To lay such seeds as may produce new vision and discovery in the years to come, this we regard as the primary task, the duty and the aim of an education worthy of its name. The task of the teacher is not to mould the mind but to enable it to grow to new dimensions—dimensions, perhaps, beyond his own reach. It is thus he serves the present for the future.

We have emphasized the ideals of a Rudolf Steiner education, but these ideals also include a meticulous care for simple and practical things, and they include the labour of overcoming difficulties. It is not merely that the new broom must sweep clean, it must sweep better than the last new broom. For example, the study of the steam engine will include not only the lives of its inventors and the obstacles they had to overcome both in the workshop and in public life, the resulting industrial revolution, the rise of new populations and their needs—it will also include painstaking draughtmanship, the basic physics required to understand what is technically involved, laboratory work, and good, clear notebooks, and (alas, for some) the unavoidable mathematics! But as a kind of compensation at least, there will be visits to industrial plants, to a locomotive shed, possibly even to a coal mine, and meetings and informal talks with the people who spend their lives in such work. Even here there may be more to learn than was altogether bargained for. I remember the young ladies of one party who chose to come out in all their Sunday best on a visit to a locomotive shed. It was an impressive sight! Well, they came out that way and they went in that way, but when they came out again—what a soiled and besooted company, but at least with purged and illumined souls! What a lifelong impression for these young people to learn from a man's own lips that he is prepared to stoke for seven long years before he can advance to become an engine driver!

Industrial visits are, for young adolescents particularly, an important part of their social education. They want to know what kind of world they live in. A single visit down a coal mine, or to an iron foundry, or to an aluminium factory opens a picture for them of modern industrial production, and also of the men and women engaged in it. To be making use of things all day long, as we do, merely as a matter of course without ever enquiring further as to who and what stands behind them is plainly egotistical. We switch on the light, we lift the receiver of the telephone, we press our foot down on the accelerator, all there for our convenience, with scarcely a thought for the human lives involved. On the other hand, such visits awaken a live interest in such matters, and with it a sense of indebtedness to all the countless human beings with their particular gifts and capacities and modes of service on whom our own lives depend. They may also help towards the realization of a persistent error in human thinking which underlies the industrial and social unrest of our times, one to which Rudolf Steiner drew attention earnestly, the idea that human labour, not just the work produced, can also be regarded as a commodity, that we can buy labour and even barter for it. Thus we confuse the value of a product which can be estimated with the inestimable character of the human gifts involved. I can pay for a pair of shoes but I can no more pay for the inventive power that designed them and the instruments involved or the skilled hands that finally shaped them than I can pay for the gift of poetry of the poet. The gifts by which human beings contribute to life can only be regarded reverently for they have their source elsewhere. To understand this, quite apart from the interest roused in the technological and practical aspects, is to nurture seeds of genuine fraternity in economic life.

We recount a visit to a glass factory and what could be seen and learnt there. First, it is surprising to know that the smooth transparency of glass is derived from sand, the ultimate crumblings of what were once crystalline rocks, hence the transparency; then to see how the sand is smelted into a liquid, that glass in its nature is a liquid—it has been found, for example, that a pane of glass in an old building is slightly thicker at the bottom, that is to say the glass, however slowly, has nevertheless been in flow all the time. The liquid glass is so very malleable but it cools quickly into the brittleness of the solid state—as though the glass is ever ready to return to its first fragmented condition from which it derives. The greatest wonder, however, was to see the glass-blowers, with their own body breath perfectly controlled, blowing the molten glass into the various shapes, here expanded, there contracted, larger or smaller at will—to perceive them with their marvellous skill and surety. They could determine, by varying their speeds of running, the relative widths of lengths of glass tubing down to a tenth of an inch or even finer. They had brought their skill right down into their legs, not only in their hands and breath. Here were craftsmen indeed, each casting a critical eye on his own handiwork before laying it aside for the next stage. Here was the pride of industry revealed at its best, in its most human aspect.

It was an old-fashioned plant, simply furnished, not too tidy, not even too clean—the work itself produced a quantity of dust which the workers must be careful not to inhale. There was an air of ease about the place though all were working hard. Pervading all was a happy mood of common interest, of fellowship, and of unstinting recognition of individual excellencies by the one for the other. The glass-blowers were gracious to the young visitors, glad to answer their questions, and the latter were impressed, in addition to all else, with the fine quality of the men's independence, each one conscious of being a *master* in his own craft.

The same class, a day or two later, went to visit a highly modernized, super-hygienic chocolate factory. Here all was faultlessly spick and span. The women were bonneted, the men capped, and all aproned in meticulous white. These same figures were seated, at set distances apart, along a moving belt with its speed-controlled motion advancing the separate chocolates; each, as a chocolate passed him or her, had a single detailed action to advance the chocolate towards its final perfection. In that situation the people seemed no more than adjuncts of a mechanical system following its own given laws, a most strange impression after the freedom of the glass-workers. As a spectacle it did not feel right. Then, at a further stage, the chocolates were placed one by one in their assigned positions in the box, the lower layer, the covering, the upper layer and more covering, and finally the lid, the assembled package, the crate for the waiting lorries and the dispatch to all the countless confectioners in this and in many other countries—an endless chain system linking an endless number of lives in this one industry organized for luxury consumption.

But there was another aspect of that factory waiting to be seen: a theatre, common rooms, musical instruments, a gymnasium excellently equipped, facilities for indoor and outdoor sports, a buffet for social occasions, and all the signs of great caring for the cultural welfare of the employees. We heard also of help with the schooling of the young, of college facilities, of care for the aged and the sick, a human counterpart to the system of automation witnessed previously. Every endeavour was being made to build up a social cultural community which, though not *visible* in the factory itself, was nevertheless there in the background, fostering a mood of warmth and fellow-feeling. There was no room for the pride of the individual craftsman, but maybe there was a shared satisfaction in the unity of purpose which pervaded the enterprise as a whole, an act of common service despite individual sacrifice.

There were questions enough to be discussed in retrospect—foremost, the picture of human beings whose daily lives were so different, yet who were all engaged in service for the greater community at large. There was born, out of these visits, a feeling of profound respect for the services rendered and of gratitude to the people engaged in them. The young people had gained one or two vivid impressions of the industrialized society we live in, and maybe a heightened sense of responsibility for the services which they themselves, in course of time, would be rendering.

We do not overlook the fact that there is much in youth that is ungainly, crude, vain, selfish and foolish—in fact, that young people *can be very trying*, as the saying is. These very things, however, are better overcome not by direct reproof but by an indirect approach—by holding up the mirror of all that the human being, in his moral being, *may* become.

Young people between fourteen and eighteen, that is, of upper school age, can be sharply critical of the adults they meet and deeply disappointed in them. The younger ones expect to be understood even in their foibles and bravadoes, and they often are not. Much of their play-acting is, after all, an attempt at asserting and testing out their growing sense of independent selfhood. They often feel badly misjudged. Why are these adults so dull, so self-contradictory, so lacking in humour? A youngster of fifteen in an American school declared in all seriousness that he knew what was wrong with the world, the adults were not really adult but only pretending to be so. Behind the assertiveness, flippancy and pointed disregard there may lie concealed great shyness, sensitivity, unsureness, even tenderness and a longing for a guiding hand which must be of their own choosing, but without which they can easily feel lost, abandoned, seeking refuge in a group or wandering off into what is often despairing loneliness. To win the confidence and affection of young people in their adolescent years is a beautiful experience for the teacher, but any direct attempt at gaining popularity will almost certainly have the opposite effect.

It is necessary for young people to be active and practical; they should make accurate as well as beautiful books; they should carve and model and paint and practise various handicrafts—for such practice activates the will, educates the feelings and develops the perceptions. Music, drama, eurythmy, play a great part, and where possible Bothmer gymnastics. These activities are educative in a high degree and very necessary. Because we live in an intellectual age, we need to pay all the more attention to educating the will and to achieving the right intensity and balance in our life of feeling.

As for the social aspect at this stage, the children in the upper school have to learn to make their own adjustments amongst themselves as well as with the specialist teachers. This stepping into the broader structure of the upper school and the encounter with a company of 'experts' in place of one constant class teacher is the best possible acknowledgement of the fact that they have entered 'into a new age of life' and that all things henceforth must be different. Their social bearing changes rapidly.

It is a frequent subject of debate amongst educators of longer standing whether the youth of today are markedly different from those of ten, fifteen, twenty years ago. Most would agree that they definitely are different and there are some who claim that they find them more intelligent, original and generally more interesting. My own experience tells me that they feel themselves to be more adult; public life has to acknowledge this. Are they not now full-blown citizens at the age of eighteen—three years of former growing towards adulthood vanished in a flash? They are certainly less bound by tradition, more adventurous (also in matters of drugs, sex, travelling, exotic teachings and practices). Yet they are also more fearfully uncertain of life, of death, of the future and, in the same degree, more sensitively perceptive and therefore more open to spiritual impressions. The ground under their feet is thin. What feeling of security can they have in a world riven by conflict and war? Will the younger generation ever see peace? The chaos of uncertainties, with old accepted standards rapidly vanishing and new standards not yet born—this reaches deeper into the soul than the mind can grasp. Life is dangerous and many young people live dangerously, and break down mentally, morally and physically. In schools and colleges they need to meet men and women who are at least one stride ahead, who are to that degree larger-minded, larger-hearted, larger-visioned, inwardly compassionate, serious at need but capable of generous-hearted laughter. If the young are different, life having so changed for them, what do we bring them that is new? By that, we mean something new to live with, new hope, new promise, new as the springtime coming out of winter.

7

WALDORF EDUCATION—IS IT
STILL NEW?

Waldorf education came into being in 1919, over two generations ago. Since then there has been the Second World War and we have fully entered into a nuclear age. This means that the balance of life on this earth is vastly changed. Children are born and grow up in conditions that have never been more precarious and unpredictable. One symptom particularly affecting childhood is the widespread disruption of family life. In view of all this it may well be asked whether Waldorf education, from its beginning, has also changed with the times. To what extent can it still be regarded as a new art of education? What is new? The fact that it is spreading faster than ever across all language barriers gives sure evidence that it is felt to belong to the present time and that it is hailed by many as having something new. On what is this based?

We know that Waldorf education is based on man as a threefold being. That he thinks, feels and wills, that he is head, heart and limb, is taken to be obvious. Even that he consists of body, mind (rather than soul) and spirit, though those terms need clearer definition, is widely accepted. Yet it can hardly be said that these distinctions have entered deeply into educational practice. There the intellectual approach has grown more dominant at all levels. Note the importance attached to the intelligence quotient (IQ test) as though the child is prominently head, and the stress on exams as the all-deciding factor. Because education is directed headwise down to the youngest children we no longer know clearly when infant becomes child, child youth, and youth adult. This in the end is not only confusing but can be disruptive.

Waldorf education, by contrast, makes a strong division between the infant years leading up to the change of teeth, the childhood years proper between the change of teeth and puberty, and the very marked changes in the youthful years following puberty. If education is clear about this, then the transitions from the one phase to the other are also clear, and the curriculum and the treatment of subjects are ordered accordingly. It is this distinction between Waldorf and other schools that struck the inspectors so forcibly.

The headwise approach, as we have called it, has serious consequences. Is the child brainy, will he be able to pass exams, are questions that weigh greatly on parents. The non-exam child, the child in whom heart and limb do not keep pace with the head, comes to be looked on as inferior. Art and the crafts play second fiddle. Thus all the three phases, infant, child and adolescent, are pressed forward intellectually and this has consequence for the whole of life. The clever ones are extolled, but where are the artists and the craftsmen who embellish life and give it greater quality? They are rare to find.

But the effects of overemphasis on head or brain learning go further than this. We see how children in the kindergarten lose their spontaneous genius for play. They grow restless, are bored or get uncontrolled, and then they need adults with their thought-out games and learning devices to engage and entertain them. What belongs properly to the first years of schooling is pushed down prematurely into the pre-school years. That means drawing children into their nervous system, making them 'heady' too soon; but that in turn also means robbing them of their early powers of imagination, the source, if allowed to play itself out naturally, of greater creativity in later life. Then, as is seen so clearly in public life, we arrive at adults who fall short of demand, who cannot enter with imagination into the problems, mainly human problems, that confront them, and therefore cannot arrive at the needed solutions. Instead they make compromises which can never be solutions. Such situations are all too familiar; that they might be the consequences of misused or misunderstood early childhood is scarcely dreamed of.

The same intellectual attitude plays as strongly into the elementary school years. We cannot wait long enough with reading, writing and arithmetic and there the slow and often more imaginative child who needs longer time comes off badly. Our public education, throughout the world, is imbued with this impatience for head-learning. Even if known, it is not accepted seriously that one is inducing prematurity of body, and therefore early puberty, or, in others, states of pre-adolescence with demands for freedom which do not belong to that age. This hinders or foreshadows the time for the healthy unfolding of heart forces, so that people later do not know how to meet one another. They tend to remain lonely, isolated figures, too caught up or engrossed in themselves. Loneliness has been described as the greatest malady of our time, leading also to excesses. There is much talk of community but little notion of sharing. So, too, parents are often at a loss to know how to meet their children.

The intellectualizing process through the school years finds its culmination in the examination system designed for the upper school. Here the examination programme with its prescribed choice of subjects, each with its given selected requirements, takes final charge of the situation, just at the time when young people are awakening to a deeper questioning of life and its meaning. They are ready to recognize and be inspired by the ideals by which others have lived and are living. They are open to appreciate the great gifts of music, poetry and art as part of themselves, and the range of love in its manifold expressions, love for the world in all its beauty and mystery—but this falls outside the requirements; there is no room for it. What matters is the exam, the only entry to higher education and the better job, it is hoped, at the end of it. By great good fortune there may be teachers, here and there, ready to share their own love and nobler aspirations with their students. This can be a precious gift running through the whole of life. One looks back to it with gratitude as an act of grace—but that is something human, beyond the system. In the main, learning for exams hinders the free unfolding of the mind.

Working from the head down instead of, as is practised in Waldorf schools, from the limbs upwards to the heart and the head, one is in danger of countering the natural devotion of the little child expressed through imitation of the adult world—that which later becomes reverence for the whole of life. So, too, we fail to engender, as we should, the refining, and healing, and joy in beauty of the elementary school years. Likewise we can so easily neglect or misread the unfolding life of imagination and the latent idealism of youth, which lends force to initiative in the years to follow. And thus we defeat, with our one-sided intellectualism, from phase to phase, the intuitive life of will, the inspirational life of feeling, and the imaginative life of thought, and arrive at a generation of depleted individuals suffering from a sense of unfulfilment and the feeling that they are not their real selves. These are the dangers. We need only look with an open eye at the world as it meets us and admit our own insufficiencies to see how inescapably true this is. It required a Huxley and an Orwell, but also many who have not written it down in books, to see the drift, through a kind of inner helplessness, towards world dictatorship in one form or another and the defeat of the free individual, which also spells an inner death.

This danger Rudolf Steiner foresaw very clearly when he was developing his ideas for a threefold commonwealth. In the broadest sense this elaborated the cry, which rang out with the French Revolution, of Liberty, Equality, Fraternity. Very briefly, these three terms could be described as three calls to all mankind: liberty of thought and culture, of each individual's different gifts and contributions; equality in the social sphere, where all stand equal before the law (what Steiner called the life of rights, where democracy has its true place); and fraternity in economic life, freed from the egotism that often attends commerce, where each person serves his fellow human beings and is in turn sustained by them—the practical ideal of each for all and all for each. These ideas are also implicit, at the educational level, in Waldorf education.

Hence to the adult he could say, extending an ancient saying, 'Know thyself in body, soul and spirit,' or, in the life of will, feeling and thought, or, going further still, in religion, art and science—in the threefold aspect of human nature, the three-in-one.

Religion as intended here is in no sense denominational but is something encompassing all humanity. So, too, art is not personal or subjective but reveals the whole of nature and creation as a work of art. By science is meant a knowledge that is all-inclusive, to which religion and art also contribute—a total survey of truth with a genuine place in it for the human being. Modern science has little place in it for man—it leaves him a homeless and lonely figure in the universe.

Turning to childhood and the goals of education, Rudolf Steiner summed up the three stages of schooling by saying:

The unconscious ideal of the young child is that the world is built on goodness.

The unconscious ideal in the elementary school years is that the world is built on beauty.

The unconscious ideal of youth is that the world is built on truth.

Thus goodness, beauty, truth are not ideals imbibed from outside but they are the inborn shaping forces of human nature. If recognized and nurtured they lead to self-realization at the highest level as the guiding principle for every human being.

These are the guiding ideals of Waldorf education, which need to be cast into a practical form that leads to practical results. To the extent that such ideals serve the future and the well-being of mankind, we may see that Waldorf education is as new and far-reaching today as on the day that Rudolf Steiner launched it into the world.

8

QUESTIONS—GENERAL AND PARTICULAR

The following are questions which recur frequently at interviews and after lectures. They will serve to illustrate a number of points connected with Steiner education which have not been dealt with in the previous pages.

The Main Lesson

The day in a Rudolf Steiner school opens with a Main Lesson which lasts approximately two hours—a very long time, it would seem, but, in the way the lessons are arranged, it passes soon enough. The Main Lesson time is devoted to the main subjects such as Mathematics, English, History, Geography, Science and so on, and these subjects are taught in block periods of three or four weeks each. This calls for further explanation.

First, with regard to the two hours. The child needs time both to receive and to give. The teacher arranges the morning period so as to allow for this. To begin with, the children will be engaged in *listening*, be it to a story, a description or whatever else is being presented as new content; there is a natural limit to this, and presently they will stand up to recite, or move round the room clapping and stamping out their tables, or do other forms of rhythmic exercise. Then, towards the end of the lesson, there comes the time when they will be found busy on some form of individual work, maybe writing, drawing, modelling or whatever the particular main lesson subject happens to require. Thus both receptive and active forces find their balance in the course of each lesson; thought, feeling and will each receive due attention, and this, in the course of years, builds up a sense of health, security and general well-being. The procedure described will vary with age and subject, but the essential aim is that all the child's faculties shall be exercised.

Each subject develops over the course of days. It is easy to observe how the experiences of the day settle into sleep, and how sleep *adds* something. Sleep is by no means merely the annulment of the day. In earlier epochs people knew this very well; they *addressed* themselves to sleep with trust and confidence—for them it was the portal of entry to those higher spheres from which they felt they derived their being and their daily strength and inspiration. Sleep leads through a positive process; the experiences of the day are carried down and established in deeper-lying regions of the soul. Through sleep, what is received during the day is woven into habits and condensed to faculties; chaotic living conditions disturb and disrupt this process. The hygiene of sleep needs to become a direct concern of education. The process of learning is an assimilative one and follows a definite course. What is absorbed through observation and thought by day sinks into deeper strata of the soul at night and returns next day to consciousness again, confirmed in feeling and in will. This is a three-day process. What is taught on one day is recalled in conversation on the second day and gathered together, written down and given its final form on the third day. What is merely apprehended on the first day returns enriched by personal feeling on the second day and becomes part of oneself by the third day. This may sound strange at a first hearing but, once attention has been drawn to it, practice will soon corroborate its truth. Of course, what is taught must engage the feelings and stir the will in the first place. But if it does, then, in the manner described, it acquires personal value and meaning for life. It is through observations of this kind that Rudolf Steiner leads education from speculative theory to specific human experience. He goes further and shows how what is taught reaches into the rhythmic functioning of the organism on the first night and into the metabolism process on the second night. The soul faculties of thought, feeling and will are directly connected with the bodily processes in the nerve and sense organization, the respiratory and circulatory system, and the system of digestion and metabolism. It is because of this intimate connection that soul impressions can so directly affect body functioning and that body conditions are so easily reflected in the life of the soul, the more so the younger the child. This three-day cycle gives an extended view of the two-hour main lesson, in which the children partly learn, partly enter into rhythm, and partly into individual work and action. It should be noted that the rhythmic element includes the art of conversation with its give and take across the classroom; Rudolf Steiner attached particular importance to this. Thus the lesson, in its organic structure, attends to head and heart and limb, and includes the fact of sleep bringing order into the life of soul. Our children today, living as they do in a welter of unrelated sense-impressions, and subject to bombardment of various kinds from the environment, *need* this help more than at any other time in history.

Added to this, continuing the same subject over a period of weeks induces a mood of quiet and cumulative concentration; it deepens learning and integrates knowledge instead of departmentalizing it—the example given earlier of the steam engine could be extended to many others.

The class teacher knows when her children have reached saturation point in a given subject and when it is desirable, therefore, to turn to a new one. She arranges the subjects over the course of the year so as to provide for the best sequence, a

more theoretical subject being followed by a more imaginative one, and so on. She also takes into consideration the
time and season of the year. The beginning of a new lesson
period becomes an event in a child's life. As text books are
rarely used, and never with young children, a new main lesson
notebook is always an exciting event. Presently it will contain
the child's own record of the new work done in class. In the
youngest classes the teacher provides most of the text and the
children illustrate. As they get older, the books become more
and more their own creations and the results are as individual
as the children themselves.

It is often asked whether, on this system of lesson 'blocks',
the children remember sufficiently what they have learned,
for the same subject may not return in this way for another
year. It is largely a question of method. If the teacher takes
the trouble, at the end of each morning, to recapitulate briefly
the ground covered that morning, the same at the end of each
week, and again at the end of the whole block period, it is
surprising how much may be recalled even after a lapse of
years. To forget for a time can also be a healthy, deepening
process. Forgetting and remembering have been likened to
going to sleep and waking again. What is recalled in memory
is no longer a merely mechanical repetition of the past but has
meanwhile been digested, assimilated and transformed
through the child's own forces. It is an ideal of this education
that the knowledge imparted should become substance for
life, that it should grow by unseen ways, like life itself, into
sustaining wisdom. If the lessons are not intellectual only, if
they are imbued with imagination, if the child has received
them gladly, if quite literally the life-blood has been stirred by
them, and if then they are allowed to sink away, to be 'forgotten' for a time, then, when recalled, they have become
experience. If, however, instead of description and char-
acterization we feed the child on definitions and ready-made

conclusions, if the object of teaching is that things should never be forgotten but should be retained in the same form all through life, we load the mind with unassimilable bodies, with stones instead of bread. The main lesson period if rightly given achieves permanence in the child's life through life itself; it *grows* and evolves with the child.

The system of main lessons continues right through the school. In the elementary school the sequence of subjects in the course of the year and the time allotted to each are matters which each class teacher works out in relation to her class. In the upper school this is taken over by the specialist teachers who work this out by mutual agreement.

Religion in our schools

Questions are often asked about religion. There are parents who fear their child may be influenced before she arrives at her own free judgement; there are others of various religious persuasions who are concerned lest their child should be alienated from them by meeting a different kind of teaching.

As for the agnostic or free-thinking parent, a realistic view of history will show that all notable forms of human culture lead back to a religious source. It follows, therefore, if child development is underpinned by human development generally, that religion must play some part in it. No child can suffer through having her thoughts and feelings raised to the highest expressions of what is good, whether in thought or picture. It is surely one of the greatest blessings in a child's life to have been able to experience reverence, devotion and awe, and to have learned to recognize how these qualities have lived in the greatest teachers of all times. Moreover, it is an illusion to think that a child can be left 'free'. The child is above all impressionable—on that all will agree. If we do not guide her positively, but leave her 'free', she merely falls subject to all the day-to-day influences that come sweeping down on her. The unmeaning and destructive nonsense which meets her everywhere then takes possession of her mind, undermining faith faster than it can be built up. There is everything to be said for children having what really belongs to them—and childhood faith, reverence and religious feeling most certainly form part of their needs.

And as for the parents with a religious concern, it may be said that the Christian attitude implicit in the life of our schools is one which includes all humanity and is in no way sectarian or bigoted. By the very fact that our history curriculum leads back to the great mythologies, we already draw near to the religions of many different peoples. The Old Testament, as was seen, has a special place even in the main lesson work. But Hinduism, Buddhism, the Muslim religion, and all that has come down from Persia, Egypt, Greece, Norse culture, ancient China, the world of America before Columbus—all these form part of the total story of man, and each is given its due. Nevertheless the Christ event in its dynamic and evolutionary aspect is regarded as the fulcrum of all that story, seen in its intimate connection with the advance to ego-consciousness typical of the whole human race. This is a view that transcends that of any particular religion, for it has room for all of them, yet pays due reverence and regard to each. Religion lessons are given in most of our schools, in some side by side with those of denominational teachers who come expressly for that purpose. In many of the schools there are also Sunday Services, taken by the religion teachers and attended by those children whose parents wish it. In the last resort, however, it is acknowledged that the question of personal religion as related to a given Church or creed belongs essentially to the home.

Circumstances differ in different countries. In the original Waldorf School, according to custom in that area, pastors of the different denominations came to the school to collect the children of their congregations for separate religious instruction. Then some of the parents approached Rudolf Steiner and asked him if their children might have special non-denominational religion lessons with teachers of the school. Thus, side by side with the already existing arrangements, there were introduced what came to be known as the 'free religion lessons'. In England the usual practice of teachers rather than pastors taking religion lessons was also followed in the Waldorf schools. In America, religious instruction is not permitted in state (public) schools, and though this restriction does not apply to private and independent schools it raises a special problem. Whatever the conditions, each school is free to make its own decision in this matter. There is no set policy of any kind.

Eurythmy

This art of movement founded by Rudolf Steiner plays an important part in all our schools. Like all the other arts, it has its special contribution. It is based on language and on tone and has been described as 'visible speech and song'.

Our poetry and music are 'flowing arts', released into space but moving in time. The plastic arts have been described as frozen music, the musical arts as form dissolved. Eurythmy makes the flow in time visible in space. Being an art, it must be exact; composed of gestures, each gesture must have precise meaning, in no way less precise than the consonant or vowel, tone or interval, which it portrays. Just as each sound of a language or each tone in music offers a great variety of nuances according to context, so has the corresponding gesture in eurythmy equal variety of expression; nothing in eurythmy is arbitrary. It is the interpretative act of the artist, subject to discipline and law, which constitutes an art. Since language is laden with thought, imbued with feeling, spun to action, eurythmy must be capable of interpreting all these; also past, present and future; epic, lyric and dramatic; the serious and the burlesque, and so on. So, too, in music, eurythmy makes visible melody, harmony, beat; major and minor; the qualities of the different keys; the mood or the changing moods of a composition; the orchestration of a piece. The training includes exercises of every kind, for skills, rhythms, alertness and sudden change, or the social interdependence of a group. Translated into classroom education, all this is excellent for children. Much that we have described as 'harmonizing' finds support and direct application in eurythmy.

Discipline

Discipline in a Waldorf school is neither rigid in the traditional sense nor free in the progressive sense. The discipline we aim for is one where there is an easy, peaceful atmosphere in which all can breathe freely. This arises quite naturally where there is the right human understanding between the teacher and her children, a caring concern met by affectionate regard. A good teacher has her own kind of discipline just as she has her own method of teaching—the two go together. Someone lacking in experience may find this a struggle for a time; if she can learn to retain her calm in class and to take herself to task at home, she is most likely to find her way; if, however, she cannot master this problem, she is probably no teacher. On the other hand where there are actual trouble makers, it becomes a question of finding and remedying the cause. Why is a certain child ill-mannered, rebellious, over-sanguine, destructive or generally provocative? The cause may lie in the home, in experiences at a previous school, or in a condition of health—bad sleep, for example—or in some

form of maladjustment either *in* the child or due to her surroundings (excessive exposure to television, for example, and,
in our view, for the young child all television is excessive).
These are matters for careful study and diagnosis on the part
of all concerned, teachers, parents, doctor. Then therapy
must follow, if possible in cooperation with the home. There
must be a cause somewhere, and this needs to be discovered.
Correction there must be, naturally—and not by mere
remonstrances but by action. Stories have often helped with
younger children (see Chapter 3). The type of action must be
suited to the child and to the offence. Sometimes a play
specially written for a child has worked wonders. Or, again, a
task carried out faithfully over a period of time, days or
weeks, in which the teacher has had the will to participate
from start to finish, may work a change for life. The following
examples will illustrate this further.

One child was reluctant to grow up; at every stage requiring
a forward step in consciousness, she held back. She was slow
with reading, number work, grammar, composition and the
rest but excelled in painting, drawing and handwork, always,
however, at a 'younger' level than her class. Socially, she was
an active, lively child, liked by her classmates, but she insisted
on remaining 'young'. At the approach to puberty, when
thought forces should grow more independent, all this took a
curious form. She longed to leave school as soon as possible.
Outside school, she began to ape the grown-ups around her
by an assiduous use of cosmetics, and her dream was to work
in a beauty parlour. Then, however, she also began to take
people's purses and to acquire in this way a private source of
wealth. When questioned about this she could, with a dis-
arming show of candour and innocence, invent the most
ingenious explanations on the spot. Her inventiveness was
extraordinary. It might have been called lying, but actually
she was only exploiting a retained gift of imagination and

fantasy beyond its normal time. She had remained too bound to her child organism; the thought forces would not release themselves. Not being able to take the forward step in thought which would have meant a real step towards growing up, she tried to compensate in other ways: she imagined herself already in the world, she painted her face in adult fashion, she began to acquire money (a perverse idea of freedom) instead of ideas. She really was innocent and a child despite her lying and her thefts. To have attempted to moralize or to punish would have been quite wrong. It was necessary to make a concerted effort to bring more activity into her thinking, not by intellectual means but through her limbs (special eurythmy and other exercises were of great help). In the two years which followed, these symptoms disappeared. When she left school, she tried out various forms of employment, discovered the way she wanted to go, and became what she had always promised to become—a bright, cheerful, warm-hearted individual who cared a great deal for others. Had she been misunderstood at a critical time, and had discipline been other than a therapy, her case might have turned out very differently.

Another child, a young boy, suffered the death of his father whom he had greatly loved. About the same time, he had a severe internal operation. He had also been trained at a former school to be ambidextrous so that he scarcely knew his right hand from his left. These various circumstances had produced a state of mental and emotional confusion and fear. His mind ran on many things but he could not concentrate, and the less he was able to do, the more despondent he became. He was witty and tried to engage his fellows by wisecracks and mischievous pranks. He could be hilarious one moment and lapse into tears the next. He had a gentle, loving disposition. In a mute way he showed his longing to be healed of his several hurts.

The German language teacher, having consulted the class teacher, decided to give him the main role in a play based on the legend of St Christopher. He was to be Offerus. Offerus was big and strong, determined to serve the strongest master. He therefore set out on a journey to find him. He was led to a mighty king and became a member of his bodyguard. Long he served him faithfully and well. Then, one day, there came a minstrel to the court. In the song he made mention of the devil. Offerus observed the king hastily cross himself with a look of fear in his eyes. So the king was not the strongest master. Offerus sought out the devil, which was not difficult. He hired himself out to the devil, wore black armour, and rode a black horse. Seven long years he served the devil faithfully and well. Then, one day, they were passing a way-side shrine, and Offerus saw the devil swerve to the side so violently that he almost fell off his horse. So the devil was not the strongest master. Offerus gave him back his black armour and his black horse and set off all over again in search of the strongest master.

One day he came to a hermitage where dwelt an ancient hermit. Offerus bowed to the hermit and said, 'Tell me, how can I find the strongest master?' The hermit replied, 'Only through fasting and prayer can you hope to find the strongest master.' Said Offerus, 'That does not suit me at all. Is there no other way?' 'Yes, there is,' said the hermit. 'Listen well, I will show you a path to follow. It will bring you to the bank of a great river. There you must build yourself a hut and dwell in it. Then, whenever anyone calls, you must carry them across the river.' So Offerus thanked the hermit, followed the path and came to the river. There he built himself a hut and lived in it and waited. Whenever anyone called he went and carried him across the river.

Years passed by and Offerus was old now, but never a sign did he have of the strongest master. One night he had lain down to rest when he heard a call. He went out to look but he saw nothing. Again he lay down to rest and again he heard a call. He rose and looked and saw nothing. Still a third time he heard the call and went out into the night. It was black, yet it seemed to him he could dimly see a child on the opposite bank. The voice calling was that of a child. Being old now he had made himself a stout staff to help him in going back and forth across the river. He now fetched his staff and went across. It was indeed a child whom he lifted on to his shoulder. As he journeyed back through the water, the child grew heavier and heavier till Offerus could scarcely take a further step. About halfway across he stumbled. 'Who art thou?' he cried. And he heard the voice say, 'Know that you are carrying on your back the whole world, and not only the world but the Lord of the world as well.' At that moment he fell forward so that his head sank below the water, and the voice continued, 'Henceforth your name shall not be Offerus. Henceforth you will be known for all time as Saint Christopher, the Christ bearer.' And so he rose, Saint Christopher, and reached and entered the hut. The child had vanished and he fell into a deep sleep. When he woke his eyes beheld growing on his old and gnarled staff a spray of pure white blossoms. Then he knew for certain that he had at last met the strongest master.

It was astonishing to see this child, at that time only nine or ten, grow into his part—how memory, confidence, clarity and strength of gesture all improved. He never turned back. By degrees he made good his deficiencies. In course of time, he himself became a teacher. It may be said that the staff of St Christopher never left his hand. He could easily have been considered a general nuisance but 'the rod' would surely not have been his cure.

The third case to be quoted is a more obvious one. It concerns a rampageous boy who had been badly pampered and spoiled and who felt himself to be no end of a lad. He could be unruly and was always showing off. It is often the pampered child who feels particularly misused and grows most critical of the adults. On one occasion this boy, in his careless boisterousness, broke an object in a classroom. This time it was the woodwork teacher who took him to task. He had him back at school several times a week for several weeks. This, in itself, had a marked effect. Why should this busy teacher be so ready to punish himself for his sake? A human contact was made. With the teacher's help, the boy constructed a difficult piece of furniture that had long been needed in the classroom. There came the day when, without comment, it was placed in position to serve the community of the whole class. This treatment, too, had an astonishing effect.

One further example, again different in kind, will have to suffice. It is not easy for a newcomer to find his way into a well-established class. This is perhaps particularly the case in a Waldorf School, where each class, continuously from year to year, becomes a well-knit unit under the aegis of the class teacher. A new arrival alters the social structure of the class. How the new member is received and integrated depends a great deal on the class teacher.

There was the case of a lad who had come from a totally different environment and who found it specially difficult to adjust. He felt he had to make his mark somehow and he did it in a very curious way: a curious art of 'spitting'. It was not that he expectorated violently in the way his grandfather might have done into the parlour spittoon. His was a far more delicate performance. At a given moment—what determined the moment was never properly discovered, unless it was that he suddenly felt forgotten—at such a moment he would purse his lips together, look around, discover his mark and fire his shot. True there was far more noise involved than actual substance, yet a modicum of substance there had to be to give support to the noise. Then he would raise his hea an expectant look in his face, wait to see what mig This was a new phenomenon in the class which too children by surprise. They, too, waited, no less, to see what might happen. What happened was that there was a silent pause and then nothing happened. This was clearly a matter of disappointment to the boy who so wanted to bring the focus of attention onto himself. He presently tried again and, indeed, a number of times and still nothing happened—possibly because the teacher himself was taken aback and did not quite know how to react. However, after a day or two of repeat performances, the teacher arrived in the morning with a large pail which he silently placed into the boy's hands. He then made a little speech about the widespread habit of spitting among certain types of animals, snails for example. Cats also have a kind of hiss and spit process when confronted suddenly by an aggressive dog—a strange mode of self-defence intended, however ineffectually, to ward off the enemy. He had also read or been told that toads spit. In the case of such animals there is always a discoverable cause, but there seems to be no evidence at all why boys should spit, certainly not in the case of a particular boy we were thinking about. Of course we would not wish to deprive him of his habit if that was going to be a real trouble to him. That is why he, the teacher, had brought the pail along for the boy's convenience. He had placed a second pail just outside the door in case it should be needed. There was only one request, that he should get it over and done with right away so as not to interrupt the lessons later. Please would he go ahead as hard as he could. Needless to say, there was not a drier mouth in the whole of Christendom. An indescribable look of surprise came into that boy's face followed by a foolish sort of grin to the giggling but good-humoured amusement of the other children. There the matter ended.

Surprise is a most valuable element in education, and, of course, humour also. As for the boy, he had his fling and came out the wiser. He turned out to be a very sweet-tempered and well-disposed individual. With the help of the teacher he had made a very good-humoured entry into the community of the class.

So one could go on. The main point is that discipline consists not only in maintaining outer order but in helping children to master their internal disorder, that it has to be therapeutic and constructive. A punishment that is to be worthwhile for the child invariably puts a burden on the teacher. A punishment that is automatic and that costs the teacher nothing has no moral value; at most it serves as a constraint—it may compel but it cannot transform. Discipline is an art which each teacher has to master in her own way.

The problem of discipline cannot be evaded. Nor does it leave room for half-measures; part-success is generally no success. The aim however must be a healing rather than a punitive one. If it is seen that despite all effort a child is not helped, parents and teachers may have to agree that a change is necessary—possibly a change of environment or even a change of school if things are really not working out, though this would be very much a last resort. There have been such instances. In any case, bad discipline is inadmissible—it is bad for the child concerned and bad for the school. Let it be remembered that the core of true discipline is willing discipleship—but this cannot be demanded, it has to be won. Experience has shown how well this form of education favours this.

It should be added, however, as a warning to all, parents and teachers alike, that conferences held in many places of late confirm the view that 'disturbed conditions' in children have much increased, partly as the aftermath of war, partly as the reflection of the disturbed conditions of the times, and partly due to the amount of distraction that besets the young. Good growing demands peace; if this is true of a plant, it cannot be less true of the human being. Where there is peace of heart and mind, peace in the home and peace in the school, the kind of discipline for which we aspire comes naturally.

Games

What is our attitude to games? Most Rudolf Steiner schools provide the customary games, though they may have their preferences. Games, however, are played as games for the exercise and fun that they provide; no special ethic attaches to them nor is the capable player selected for special hero-worship. She is admired for her good achievement as is the good craftsman, the good actor, the good musician, the good at anything; no disgrace to one who cannot play. There are children with a natural dislike for organized games and they should be considered too and a suitable alternative found for them. But our children, when they do play, are known to play well and generally hold their own against competitors. They carry into their games the poise, agility and enthusiasm won from other activities.

It is often said that games provide a necessary outlet for the will; to the extent that this is true, it applies to our schools where the children have so much more scope for creative activity. Be that as it may, the simple fact remains that most children like games and should be able to have them, within reason and under good conditions. In so far as games are played at all in a Waldorf School, for the sake of the general morale it is important that teachers should learn to take a genuine interest in them and share in the enthusiasm of the children. Resentment grows in the children if teachers hold aloof and merely allow games to go on. They can, however, also be over-stressed, and have excessive ethical values attached to them. To learn to 'play the game' should be as simple as the words denote. Riding, swimming, boating and other such sports are encouraged where possible—also general outings and camping.

Transfer to another school

Parents wishing to enter their children into a Waldorf School are sometimes concerned about what would happen if they had to leave the district and their children had to go to another type of school. Would they find themselves at a disadvantage?

At the outbreak of the war, Michael Hall was evacuated from London to Somerset and lost a hundred children. Some of these children could be followed up later. The general pattern was much the same. Not having been drilled in the usual intellectual way, and having followed a curriculum which does not run parallel to that in other schools, some of these children found themselves, to begin with, at a disadvantage. Then, however, their freshness and liveliness of interest took over and most of them got on surprisingly well.

Again, before the Rudolf Steiner School in New York had its own High School, children left at the seventh or eighth grade or even earlier for entry to the high school of their choice. Their record of achievement was greatly encouraging. With few exceptions they did very well, often even better than might have been expected of them.

The reason is the same. This education releases capacities, keeps the mind and imagination fresh, and wakens life interests. These qualities the children take with them wherever they go; they mark them out as good students.

Transfer from another school

How late do you take children into your schools? The answer to this is: up to almost any age depending on the child. Though naturally the younger the better, there have been instances of children joining as late as the tenth or even the eleventh class who have quickly found the school to be their home and done well in it. Children who have had an over-intellectual education may, for a time, seem to lose their bearings; they do not know how to gauge the type of self-discipline, both in behaviour and in work, which is required of them. Help is needed here. In the main, the new type of demand and the relationship which exists between teacher and child bring happiness and release. Much that was previously unused is called into play. Often it is the late new-comers who appreciate what the school means to them better than do others who might never have been to any other type of school. It is not a question of doubting the excellence to be found in other schools, but rather of pointing to the fact that the understanding for the child and her needs is different.

Entry into life

It is sometimes feared that children from these schools might find it specially difficult to adjust to life as it ordinarily is today. Are the ideals in our schools perhaps unsettling for the tough business of everyday life?

Experience has proved the contrary. It is true that first experiences of a harsh world may, sometimes, come a little hard, but old scholars have shown themselves very well able to meet difficult and shifting circumstances, to retain their presence of mind under stress, and to take initiative in the situations which they meet.

At a discussion amongst old scholars about what their

education has done for them, one of them declared: 'In my opinion, the education I received has definitely made life harder rather than easier, but this is just what I would not wish to have missed for it has taught me what real living means.'

Speaking generally, the old scholars of these schools are open-minded and much interested in the world around them and in people. Out of their human interest, they are ready to strike in when needed rather than remain aloof. Because they feel the problems of others and see their needs, they are the more ready to intervene helpfully and to take on responsibilities which may bring burdens but which make life real. Perhaps this is what that particular old scholar meant.

It is hard for anyone to know what she might or might not have been had this or that influence not affected her. There are countless people who have all the good qualities we have described and it cannot be said by any means that all old scholars possess them. Waldorf education does not create these qualities but it certainly sets out to serve them. There is no doubt that the imaginative approach of the earlier years translates itself into insight and initiative later and that the reverence for the world which is cultivated leads to a heightening of social responsibility. It is also true that Steiner education sets out to foster a balanced outlook which mitigates political and other forms of fanaticism, stressing purely human values.

For whom are these schools intended?

Is this education specially adapted for Europeans? Is it as good for others?

This education is born from a new view of the human being and is intended for human beings the world over. It bears an international character; that is why it has spread to so many lands already and continues to spread.

An Indian educator, a lady, once visited a Waldorf School in England. It was explained to her that one of the endeavours of the education was to hold back over-rapid intellectual development and instead to encourage greater imagination. Her comment was interesting. It appeared to her that this same education applied in India could serve in the opposite way, namely, to counter the tendency to remain too long suspended in images and to bring the intellect to birth more quickly. She thus gave tribute both to the universality and the ready adaptability of this education.

Today, through the initiative of a courageous man and his wife (Indians who had each spent some time at Emerson College[1] and visited Waldorf Schools not only in England but in Norway, Holland, Switzerland and Germany), there are a number of nursery-kindergartens, Waldorf in type, and a school in Dalhousie. This is pioneering work which needs and deserves all the help it can get, not least through visits of Waldorf-trained teachers to help and train further native teachers that are there.

In South America there is a Waldorf School of a thousand children at Sao Paulo in Brazil, as well as three others; there are two schools in Argentina, two in Colombia, one in Peru and in Uruguay and an initiative in Mexico.[2]

In our intellectual West we tend to set the same kind of standard for all peoples and for all the individuals of any one nation. That is why our theories so easily come unstuck where human relationships are concerned. But man is so much more than a speculative brain. However useful and necessary the intellect may be, the forces which guide life lie much deeper. It is in these depths that we have our true being and it is out of these depths that mutual understanding must come.

Examinations

It will have become clear that the type of work needed for examinations falls outside the primary aims and intentions of a Waldorf School. The examinations required for entering college or professional training courses, far from forming our culminating work, invade and compromise the curriculum of our upper classes. Where the examination pressure grows acute, there may easily arise conflict between the immediate and so-called practical results of examinations and the ultimate and truly practical results at which this education aims. Each school, within the compass of its given possibilities, tries to arrange its programme as best it can to meet both the immediate and the ultimate ends. In general it can be said that the examination results in our schools compare well with those in other schools. Less time is spent on this work than elsewhere; on the other hand, to safeguard the Waldorf curriculum as far as possible, the examinations are generally taken later. The sacrifices involved in keeping a child that much longer at school should be weighed against the benefits of doing so spread over a whole lifetime.

Perhaps something further needs to be added, for indeed the question of examinations cannot be glossed over—it affects the lives of children so directly, and their parents also. There is such a deep-rooted bias towards intellectual things. A class in which children have worked and grown in happy harmony for years, confronted suddenly with the examination problem, falls apart into those who can, those who might, and those who cannot. This is a matter of real distress and results in a totally false evaluation of human merits. There are Steiner Schools which have set up, parallel to the examination class, a whole department in arts and crafts running courses up to apprenticeship level, with excellent results, but still the prejudice persists that anything that falls short of the academic must somehow be inferior. Today, many a college graduate walks about with hands in pockets, forced to live on the dole through lack of employment, while real craftsmen are harder and harder to find.

What is the examination—that is, the school leaving exam—in reality? The syllabus is fragmentary and superficial. In examinations little more is demanded than a recapitulation of prescribed facts. To the extent that some degree of thinking is called for, it is still the standard answer, pre-established in the mind of the examiner, that scores highest. Originality is neither looked for nor expected. Everything is supposed to be 'objective'. In the last resort, the Yes-No type of computerized test is the most objective of all! There, even the examiner becomes unnecessary, and matters are entirely depersonalized. Yet it is such examinations alone which offer the means of entry to colleges and the professions.

How different is the case with some of the older universities where the main importance attaches to a three-hour essay on a subject chosen there and then out of a given list for which there could have been no previous preparation. The subjects listed are all concerned with broad aspects of life and knowledge. Here the examiner's main interest is to discover whatever is unique in mind and expression in the young applicant. Originality of thought and imagination are actually sought. Here is a condition of what might be called *human* objectivity and true regard for culture.

The trend has gone far away from this. Yet, since action and reaction are a real part of life, there are signs of a new liberality arising here and there, reaching towards a freer and more enlightened outlook. It is not too much to say that dry and pedantic over-intellectualism is threatening to be the death of us and of nature too. It is high time to recognize that the human being is endowed with a threefold nature in thought, feeling and will, and nothing short of attention to all three will do. Therefore, a young person, if she is to be tested at all, should in justice be tested in all three: she should be given an opportunity to reveal her powers of thought, so, too, her capacity for artistic appreciation and expression, and, not least, evidence of her ability to handle a practical skill. There would then be a basis for a balanced assessment of all three faculties and how best to advise each person on her further course. This would go a long way to abolishing the false scale of values which prevails today. We might then learn to honour head, heart and limb in equal measure, all three making up a total human being.

That is precisely what is striven for in Waldorf Schools, where the teachers unite in their endeavours to build up a truly objective picture of each child both for the children themselves in a way appropriate to their age and for their parents. This way no formal examinations are called for or found necessary. The nearest approach to such freedom in procuring formal recognition and the granting of a public certificate has occurred in a number of schools, notably in Germany. The teachers in these schools are able to set their own examination based on their own syllabus of requirements. They also do their own invigilating in the familiar school premises, the only proviso being that a representative of the educational authorities should be in general attendance. This is the most human situation that has offered itself so far. Such schools are truly privileged and all concerned can be grateful. Here is a situation, essentially human, based on trust.

Competition

Since we do not encourage competition, how are our children prepared to enter a competitive world?

Stronger than the spirit of competition is the spirit of emulation, the readiness to appreciate what is admirable in others, and therefore worthy of being striven for. Thus each is encouraged to do better. The only worthwhile competition is with oneself, to outgrow what one is in striving, to become what one might be. That is the spirit above all which needs to be encouraged. It is then not a question of whether or not one is better than another but whether one is oneself at one's best. Emulation becomes a powerful force in life, a moral and redeeming force, whereas competition has no mercy for the weaker and breeds egotism.

A teacher has endless opportunities to draw the attention of her children to the happy use of a word, a phrase or an image in someone's composition, or maybe a striking use of colour, or a commendable point of behaviour—*something* to be justly extolled now in the one child, now in another. In an exhibition of class work no one is ever left out, and so it is in daily life. A child who is known to have had a difficulty, and who then, by dint of great effort, is able to surmount it is a matter of rejoicing for the whole class. That is what difficulties are for, to be surmounted, and thereby we grow.

Emulation encourages charity of heart, something much needed at all times, and leads to a future society born in fellowship. Competition, as can be seen all too easily in our 'competitive world', hardens people into an attitude of each for himself before all else. One is led to believe that conquest is through force, but such conquest always fails. One can also conquer through the gift of love which is ready to make room for another. Such conquest has in it something far more abiding.

There is no point in moralizing in these matters but of only recognizing the truth. The educator, if she is true to her task, is concerned with that 'greater strength' in us beyond the competitive. It is, after all, ideals we have to serve, and one so easily falls into the error of seeing the ideal as something unreal, whereas it is in fact the very life-blood of education.

9
TO PARENTS

Parents will have their own reasons for choosing to send their children to a private school. No doubt they will have made careful enquiry into the character of the school and the particular benefits it offers. That this should be the case in connection with Waldorf Schools is highly desirable, for the life of these schools depends to a great degree on close understanding and cooperation between parents and teachers. It needs to be understood that what is offered in these schools is not the product of just another educational theory but is based on a total view of life that encompasses religion, art, science, history, reaching into the very heart of what we might come to see as the real foundation of knowledge and life on earth. Rudolf Steiner himself said that the Waldorf Schools would grow because they were seen to be good schools, that is, schools that do good to children. That was the basis on which Michael Hall received official recognition. The inspectors did not feel they needed to enter into the philosophy of the school—they judged by what they saw to be its fruits, and to a large extent that is the case with many of the parents. Yet there are always some who want to pursue things further. The question has been asked, for example, whether, since all the teachers serve a common ideal, there might not be some danger of indoctrination.

Once we have come to acknowledge the fact that education down to the most elementary levels is dominated by tenets of materialistic science, we may also readily see that we are already indoctrinated from the start by a one-sided view of the human being and the world; moreover one that undermines human values and is leading to wholesale havoc in public and in private life. The very triumphs of our advancing technology have multiplied disaster and have overwhelmed humanity with threats and anxieties on a fearsome scale. Waldorf teachers take full account of the positive achievements of our time, but they also perceive the moral as well as the material dangers that are invading life. They strive to develop a view both of nature and of human nature which includes the moral with the physical, correcting the one-sidedness of materialism. Then, instead of being mere onlookers at a world which, as is supposed, could go on just as well without us, we become an integral part of the whole of creation, bringing new meaning to all that comes to meet us. It becomes natural, as Rudolf Steiner proposed, that the human being should hold a central place in every subject taught. What the school is doing, far from indoctrinating, is to provide a corrective to the severe indoctrination which is already taking place, influencing every moment of our lives, and determining the future in which our children must play their part. It is a blessed thing for children if parents and children can enter into a mutual understanding of this.

Let us carry this somewhat further. The world is presented as being ruled by number. The eighteenth century view that mathematics is the key to the universe still largely prevails. Let us take the simple example of a piano. The construction is most certainly ruled by number, but in so far as the piano is an instrument for music, the numbers are subject to the indefinable laws and realities of the art of music. A skilled musician is needed to reveal what the piano is actually meant to be. Slowly, very slowly as yet, such a view is beginning to dawn in relation to the whole of creation. Number is there, and structure is there in mineral, plant, animal, man, in physics, chemistry and all the sciences, number in the proportions to be met in art as well as nature, number in all the rhythms that permeate all nature, above all, living nature—number is there not as the *cause* but as the revealed *consequence* of what rules in creation. Our science has arrived at a quantitative view of the world in which quality, beauty in nature and human morality become uneasy presences. The world is viewed as a machine and the human being as an inconsequent cipher. Clearly if this view is to persist, it can only bring ruin in its wake. We have to find a way, a *scientific* way, of arriving at the perception of the world as a meaningful work of art, and of man as the bearer of a new evolving morality, in his unceasing striving for truth, beauty, wisdom, love.

In this endeavour, born of the life-long work of Rudolf Steiner, a Waldorf School, if rightly understood, stands in the forefront of genuine progress towards a saner future. The work is bound to prosper to the extent that parents, out of their own life experience, come to see the truth of this. Then any fear of indoctrination must simply fall away, and the work be seen as one that is intended to help free human faculties from their present bondage to a materialistic world view.

Our older children are not aware of the fact that in many respects they are being taught differently from children elsewhere. On one occasion a group of sixteen-year-olds, who had been brought up mainly in a Waldorf School, approached a teacher with the following direct questions. 'We would like to know what you have been teaching us. For example, you have often spoken to us of the threefold human being. We would like to know whether what you have been teaching us is what you think, or what Dr Steiner thinks, or what the world thinks.' The teacher answered somewhat as follows: 'What I have taught you is what I think, but in arriving at the thoughts I have shared with you I was very much helped by the thoughts of Rudolf Steiner. It is not the way the world in general thinks today. But of this I can fully assure you: you will have no difficulty in understanding what you will be taught at college of the way the world thinks, but you may recall that there is another possible approach to the same phenomena.

'Now who will be in a better position to form a free judgement, he who has met only the one dominant view, as expressed in textbooks, or someone who will be in a position to compare this with at least one other point of view?'

There was a pause, and then one of the young company, a choleric, thumped his chest and said, 'Mr X. I declare myself thoroughly satisfied.'

Many years later most of that group met the same teacher again. This same student, now well established in his profession, asked: 'Are you not disappointed, Mr X., that so few of us have followed your point of view?'

And Mr X. replied, 'No, I am not disappointed. My object was not that you should follow my point of view, but that you should be better able to arrive at your own.'

Looking back over the years, the young people of the first interview, now entering middle age, could agree that far from being subjected to dogma or being indoctrinated, they had been prepared for a life of inner freedom in which they could find themselves and decide their own views.

One cannot be long acquainted with a Waldorf School without hearing of Rudolf Steiner and his teaching which he called anthroposophy. People find it a puzzling word. It actually combines two words, *anthropos*, man, as in anthropology, and *sophia*, wisdom, as in philosophy. In other words: wisdom about the human being. Man, we will admit, is still the greatest mystery we can meet on earth, and wisdom we know to be something other than knowledge. A wise person is one who has insight, one who can see life from within. A fuller interpretation of the word anthroposophy might be spiritual insight into the world as revealed through the nature of the human being. An American professor once wrote: 'In these days of exploration of outer space is it not necessary that we also begin an exploration of inner space?' That is precisely what anthroposophy sets out to do, but whereas from outer space we make use of many outer instruments, for inner space we ourselves must become the instrument, that is, we have to develop further the faculties with which we are already endowed, that is, our thinking, feeling and willing. There are words in common usage which point in the direction of such a development. We say of someone that he has a powerful imagination; of another that he is greatly inspired; of a third that he is profound in his intuitions. All three words, Imagination, Inspiration, Intuition, carry the mind beyond the everyday. Anthroposophy offers disciplines enabling anyone who has the will to develop these faculties, possessed by all human beings in varying degree, into higher organs of perception. In the past we have lived very much by the gifts of the chosen few. Today, each one of us, as modern human beings, can strive in some measure to join their ranks, if only in the sense of taking full responsibility for our lives.

That is what the teacher meant who said to that group of children that he teaches as *he* thinks, not as he has been told to think, even though he admits his great indebtedness to Rudolf Steiner. The age of authority in the old sense has gone. It is because human beings do not sufficiently realize this and therefore fail to find the authority within themselves that the world is largely falling subject to all manner of external controls, so that one begins to wonder whether the age of human freedom will ever come. Our romantic poets thought the French revolution had opened the way to it with the cry, 'Liberty, Equality, Fraternity', but they were sorely disappointed. They had to learn that freedom has to come from within and that it is inseparable from the power of love.

Thus Coleridge, still young, aged only twenty-five, could write:

> ... on that sea-cliff's verge,
> Whose pines, scarce travelled by the breeze above,
> Had made one murmur with the distant surge!
> Yes, while I stood and gazed, my temples bare,
> And shot my being through earth, sea, and air,
> Possessing all things with intensest love,
> O Liberty! my spirit felt thee there.

Do we teach anthroposophy? No, we do not, but we try to teach in such a way that children and young people can find their way towards the fullness of an experience such as that of Coleridge—that it may open ways, within the grasp of each one, to develop his inner life, and therefore also advance his outer life. Education can help achieve this. Parents can surely help achieve it too. The first years of a child's life, before even kindergarten begins, are entirely in their hands. This responsibility goes right back to the moment of birth and even before. Surely every child that comes into this world must have an annunciation similar to that of the archangel Gabriel to Mary. The warm, welcoming thoughts of parents have a deep effect on the unborn child. And then so very much depends on the environment created, first the love that streams to the child, but an informed love that also knows how to attend to outer conditions; the right degree of light, of warmth, the right colours on the walls for the very young child; the right diet when the time comes (our doctors advise against meat in the early years); the right regularity of habits, waking to each day with a song and a prayer, and even more so when settling down to sleep; and the right toys, simple, colourful, *not* mechanical, not porcelain dolls that shut their eyes, and so on. These first years are the most deeply impressionable in the whole of life. The child, says Rudolf Steiner, is one great sense organ, absorbing every impression. Young parents need to study these things and, if need be, seek help and advice.

Then, when the child goes to the nursery or kindergarten, parents can again observe, consult, bring the home life into harmony with what the child receives at school. What shall the child best wear as the year goes round, especially in the winter to protect body warmth?

And then come the eight years with the class teacher—one great continuous adventure. It is above all important that parents should not merely accept what the school does and gives but they should *know why* reading is introduced later, feeling assured of the rightness of this—the why and the when and the how of everything done; the parents have a right to know, and the teachers will be happy to share, to consult and be consulted. Childhood is not merely a succession of years; each year is different and there are also *crisis years*, times of special change which need to be well understood.

And then come the upper school years. It is not only that the children enter the upper school having left their class teacher. Puberty brings problems, and adolescence demands a change of relationship with parents as well as with teachers and the adult world generally. These are real changes. The fact that some changes come earlier nowadays means there is a need for further study and understanding to be shared by parents and teachers, increasingly involving the children also. A Waldorf School provides a learning and growing situation not only for the children but for parents and teachers as well.

There are, of course, many ways in which parents can enter more closely into the social and cultural life of a Waldorf School, opportunities not only to study but to be introduced also to the arts, maybe to eurythmy, to painting, to music. Then there are festival occasions and exhibition times when parents can have a survey not only of their own children's classes but of the whole school. There is usually a parent-teacher association. There is a great need for pioneer parents as well as pioneer teachers to carry the whole Waldorf movement further into the world, so that the benefits of this education may reach the greatest possible number of children. We need parents who can articulate to others what Steiner education is all about.

A lot of work for all, but we hope a joyous work!

10

THE FORM AND ORGANIZATION OF A WALDORF SCHOOL

A Rudolf Steiner or Waldorf School is co-educational throughout. It is not merely that boys and girls are taught together and that men and women share the work alike. The aim is so to educate through art that it may bring new life to science and so to educate through science that it may bring greater consciousness to art. True co-education consists in establishing the right relationship between these two, between feeling penetrated with thought and thought permeated with feeling, and for this it is most fitting to have the sexes grow up side by side. In the past, the ideal of the man was to be out-standingly male, the ideal of the woman to be completely female. In the individualized society of today this is no longer so. The male needs to acquire some of the qualities which in the female yield plasticity of soul, the female needs equally to gain those qualities which in the male lead to greater clarity and independence of thought. It has become a commonplace to talk of the equality of the sexes. This does not deny the reality of differences between the sexes but points rather to a society of the future which will rest more and more upon those intrinsic human qualities which reach beyond male and female. Signs of this are to be seen everywhere. The relationship between men and women in public life is very different from what it was fifty years ago. That this change can best be served by co-education only the diehard few of yesterday will care to question.

Waldorf Schools take children right through from the age of three or four to eighteen or nineteen, for childhood is viewed as a progressive whole, though with well-defined phases as described previously. So connected are the three great periods of childhood that to cut through them wilfully is like cutting into life itself. It is good for older children to recall their own earlier years in the younger children round them and good for the younger children to glimpse something of the years which lie ahead as they look towards the older children. One of the most interesting and impressive innovations in a Waldorf School is the monthly or termly children's festival. Children throughout the school present examples to the rest of the school of work they have done in class, recitation in their mother tongue and in foreign languages, flute playing, singing, a play they have prepared, a scene out of the history lessons, a demonstration from the science class, a piece of eurythmy or some of their gymnastic exercises, and so on. It is at such a festival that the corporate unity of the school is experienced powerfully. As for the teachers, their continued association in work which covers the whole range of these years develops insights into childhood life and growth as nothing else can.

A Waldorf School takes its form from the fact that all three periods of childhood are included. The very little children, before they enter the school proper, form a self-contained community in themselves. Then comes the succession of eight classes, each with its own class teacher. These classes are referred to by the name of the class teacher and only rarely by number. Finally, there is the upper school with its circle of specialist teachers. The same plan holds good for the larger schools with their parallel classes.

There are no prefects with badges and no set appointments. The feeling of seniority comes from the changing relationship with the teachers and amongst the students themselves and particularly from the work in the classroom, the problems discussed, the tasks which are given and the demands made.

The exercise of leadership is not overlooked, but instead of having a system with fixed appointments and hierarchies it is called upon as actual needs and situations arise. Since these are bound to vary, different children have opportunities given them to serve in different ways according to their gifts and capacities. In this way life is kept in continuous flow. As given demands arise, the capacity to meet them springs into place; there is no rigid pattern. Some question this until they see its greater virtue. They would prefer formal appointments, rules, rewards and punishments. This evades the problem of self-discipline; yet command over self, not command over others, is the first prerequisite of any free society. Genuine authority cannot be taught, it has to be engendered. Therefore, contrary to the methods of self-government practised in other schools, in a Waldorf School final authority rests solely with the adults, though consultative meetings between teachers and the older scholars have now become customary—indeed they are seen to be essential for the happy conduct of an upper school.

In a Waldorf School there is not the same need as elsewhere for a headteacher. The nursery class teacher represents the school to the parents of the children in her care. Each class teacher quite obviously takes prime responsibility for her class and is best suited to deal with the parents of her children. Each specialist teacher is similarly responsible for her department; they work things out together. Upper school parents may consult whom they will, though, for routine purposes, it has been found useful for each upper school class to have one teacher as a class adviser or counsellor. All the teachers with their different spheres of responsibility meet together as a body, and it is this collective body which has the final direction of the school. The body of teachers, often referred to as college of teachers (really the colleagueship of teachers), appoints its own chairman, executive, and whatever other functionaries may be needed. Such appointments are more in the nature of delegations taking account of the special gifts and capacities which the one or other may have to serve the whole. The personnel engaged changes from time to time. This method of delegation makes for continuity in the work and yet for greater freedom for the teachers. A teacher will undertake the task that it seems best for her to undertake at a given time. At another time she may be able to serve best in another way. On the other hand, the character of the school need never depend on any one individual or group of individuals; the essential character will be maintained by the directing body of teachers even if, in course of time, the individuals comprising that body should totally change.

The teacher body carries all ultimate responsibility for the school but it generally has an advisory body of governors or trustees and administrative office staff.

Finally it should be added that Waldorf Schools are independent entities, each responsible for itself and its own maintenance. There is friendly cooperation between schools but no central organization to rule over them. The only ruling principle is the work which is common to them all, the uniting factor being the study of the child in the light of Rudolf Steiner's deep wisdom as has been briefly outlined in these pages.

11

THE RANGE OF RUDOLF STEINER'S WORK FOR CHILDREN

Rudolf Steiner education has also become associated with children with various types of learning difficulty. The work for these children has developed magnificently since its first inception, some few years after the founding of the original Waldorf School in 1919; its very success has led to certain misconceptions which it is our purpose to correct here.

It was Rudolf Steiner's view that schools founded on his methods should gain ground simply through their recognition as *good schools*. Their progress has been of this kind. It was quickly found, however, that the methods used were of great benefit to many children who were otherwise in difficulties. Very soon, children began to come recommended by doctors, psychologists, child guidance clinics and educational authorities; grateful parents spread their good news further and all this gave rise to the idea that these schools could deal with special cases—indeed, that they were in some way special schools. Thus, what was good news in the first place turned to error. The question of the 'problem' child is a widespread and difficult one. A lecture on such children will always draw large audiences.

Rudolf Steiner was approached from several quarters for advice about badly retarded and sick children, including Down's syndrome, epileptics, hysterics, spastics, hydrocephalics, schizophrenics and others. As a result *homes* for such children began to spring up, notably in Germany, Switzerland, Holland and England (later in Scotland also). Men and women came forward with great and noble zeal to throw themselves heart and soul into this work, and their attitude to these children, inspired by Rudolf Steiner's teaching, became something very new. The children were regarded not merely as 'unfortunates' but, out of deepened understanding of human destiny, as sufferers for the human race, bearers of the widespread ills of mankind focused on themselves. Far from being mere recipients, they were looked upon as a moral challenge to our times. The intellect can serve them little; quite other forces, the most deeply human of which we are capable, are called into action—for treatment not born of profound devotion and love is of little avail for such children. This work, also carried on in the name of Rudolf Steiner, has grown splendidly and is constantly discovering new ways and means; in it the ideals described in these pages are brought to the most needy and sick. Such centres may well be called 'homes', for these seemingly helpless ones have no *home* elsewhere on this earth, and in these homes where they are met with spiritual understanding their happiness is marvellous to behold.

Mention may here be made of the Camphill Movement founded by the late Dr Karl König and now a world movement in its own right. It comprises 'The Camphill Rudolf Steiner Schools for Children in Need of Special Care', training facilities for work with such children, and also a number of Camphill Villages, run as working community centres for mentally handicapped young people and adults.

It became apparent that there was a wide range of children not catered for either by the Waldorf Schools for normal children, or by the Rudolf Steiner Schools and Homes for special needs children. Such children were loosely described as 'maladjusted'—which could mean emotional or behavioural disturbances, or generally undernourished and underdeveloped in their mental, moral and social being. Such children also needed the utmost 'special care'—educational, medical, social and environmental—to bring them into better harmony in themselves and with their fellows, and, when older, a training in some craft to help them find their way into the main stream of life. A number of Rudolf Steiner centres have come into being, mostly in Great Britain, generally described as 'Home Schools', to address these particular needs.

We may see how the name of Rudolf Steiner has become associated with every imaginable type, phase and condition of childhood. In this he stands unique in the field of education. He died in 1925 but the work he began continues to grow, expand and find ever new ground. There are, today, over six hundred Waldorf Schools in the world, even more children's homes, as well as the 'Home Schools'. All these are based on the fundamental ideas about child development described here.

12

THE WALDORF SCHOOL MOVEMENT

Waldorf education dates back to September 1919, when the first Waldorf School was founded by Rudolf Steiner himself. This took place in Stuttgart in Southern Germany at the request of the then director of the Waldorf Astoria cigarette company in that city. The school was intended in the first place for the children of the factory employees, thus arising directly out of modern industrial life. The school grew in leaps and bounds to the size of a thousand children, drawing its pupils from many parts of Germany, from other countries in Europe and even from as far away as America. In the years that followed ten other schools were founded in Germany. Hitler declared that the philosophy in these schools with its emphasis on nurturing individuality ran contrary to that of National Socialism, and therefore they must close. During the war years therefore, this left some half a dozen small strug-gling schools in Switzerland, England and North America. There was little or no communication between them and the outlook was extremely bleak.

Immediately after the war ended, the schools began to revive, to grow and multiply almost too quickly for there to be sufficient teachers trained in Waldorf methods. There are schools today throughout the world. The spread of schools has come about through no kind of central plan or directive. On the contrary, each school is an entirely independent enterprise, resting wholly on the initiatives of teachers and parents and whatever local support they may find. It is in this way alone that a worldwide Waldorf movement has come about, purely on the merits of the work itself and what it offers. Every such school entails great commitment on the part of teachers, parents and friends. Nevertheless the work continues to grow, more easily in countries such as Denmark, Germany, Norway and, to some extent, Holland and Finland in Europe, and also Australia and New Zealand, where the governments do in a measure subsidize private education. This, unhappily, is not the case in Britain, Canada, the United States and elsewhere.[1] Yet there are still numerous schools in these countries, with more opening all the time.

Rudolf Steiner gave the first suggestions for education as far back as 1907, but an actual request for a school did not come until human conscience had been stirred to the uttermost by the fearful calamity of the First World War. This left all thinking people stunned, with a sense of moral and social failure and the collapse of all the alluring hopes people had been nursing for a forthcoming era of assured peace, industrial progress and economic security on an ever-widening scale. The phase that followed that war period was one of dictatorships which, in turn, led directly into the Second World War.

Today we are floundering in a morass of doubts and uncertainties with new horrors in the headlines every day. All this gives evidence of a fact that few can fail to recognize: that we find ourselves entangled in the decaying elements of an old world order with its traditional faiths and authorities, and that the world awaits the birth of a new faith, a new vision, and a new conscience, a new awakening to the reality of man as a spiritual being. How can we rediscover ourselves and, in so doing, find that despite all the frantic contradictions of the times, the sustaining forces of all existence are still the realities of truth, beauty, goodness which find their fulfilment in love? It is out of renewed knowledge of the human being, a knowledge imbued with wisdom, (Anthropos-Sophia) that Waldorf education has been born.

Waldorf education directs itself to the growing forces of the child, to the ground of human morality perceived in the healthy life of play of the infant years, to the ground of social being expressed in the healthy life of feeling in the childhood years, to the ground of mutual understanding based on a healthy enhancement of thinking in the adolescent years, so that the young adult, when he comes to himself, may find himself at home in the world. Since these are actual needs and not inventions, more and more people are learning to recognize in Waldorf education a means to enable children, through the right engaging of their faculties in the ordered sequence of the years, to grow into a generation of men and women with more likely answers to the world situation than people have today. The future must lie in the maturing forces of childhood which carry within themselves the mystery of human evolution. The task of education is to nurture these forces so that they may find their truest possible expression in the years to come, in individual and in public life.

13

WALDORF TEACHER TRAINING

People often ask: 'How do you find your teachers?' The most obvious answer is: 'Life brings them.' The teachers we meet in the Waldorf Schools are men and women who found their way to them in the course of their search for enlightened human values and out of a deep concern for our social future. Some were teachers already before they heard of Waldorf Schools and Rudolf Steiner. Others, finding anthroposophy, were inspired to become teachers. There are several centres today which offer special training in Waldorf methods. In broad terms the following are the elements of training common to them all:

A study of the threefold nature of the human being as body, soul and spirit.

A detailed study of child development in all its phases including a particular study of the temperaments.

The Waldorf curriculum and its intimate relationship to the forces of growing childhood in infancy, the elementary school years and adolescence.

Storytelling and story making, also for remedial purposes.

Tutorial courses in basic subjects such as mathematics, literature, history, history of art, music, the sciences, etc.

Ongoing practice of the arts: weekly classes in speech and eurythmy and block periods in painting and modelling; also optional classes in recorder playing, crafts and, where this can be provided, in Bothmer gymnastics.

Classroom observation and practice teaching.

Organizational aspects, parent-teacher relationships, medical questions, etc.

The following are the best known and the longest established of the Waldorf Teacher Training Centres, though as the Waldorf Movement continues to grow and expand new centres are opened up. No list can be up-to-date for very long but further information is always available on enquiry. At many of these centres there is a preliminary year of study and artistic work, comparable to the Foundation Year at Emerson College, before proceeding to educational studies proper.

England
Emerson College, Forest Row, Sussex, RH18 5JX.

USA
Rudolf Steiner College, 9200 Fair Oaks Boulevard, Fair Oaks, CA 95628.

Waldorf Institute of S. California, 17100 Superior Street, Northridge CA 91325.

Waldorf Institute, 260 Hungry Hollow Road, Spring Valley, New York 10977.

Antioch University, Antioch/New England Graduate School, Roxbury Street, Keene, NH 03431.

Switzerland
Lehrerseminar, Brosiweg 5, CH 4143 Dornach.

Germany
Seminar für Waldorfpädagogik, Haussmannstrasse 44A, D-700 Stuttgart 1.

Institut für Waldorfpädagogik, Annener Berg 15, D-5810 Witten-Annen.

Freie Hochschule für anthroposophische Pädagogik, Zielstrasse 28, D-6800 Mannheim 1.

Lehrerseminar für Waldorfpädagogik, Brabantestrasse 43, D-3500 Kassel-Wilhelmshöhe.

There are also seminars in Hamburg, Heidenheim, Hiel and Nuremberg.

Sweden
Rudolf Steiner Seminariet, S-15300 Järna.

Kirstofferseminariet, Box 124, S-16126 Bromma.

France
Perceval Pédagogie Rudolf Steiner, 5 rue Georges-Clemenceau, F-78400 Chatou.

Netherlands
Vrije Pedagogische Akademie, Socrateslaan 22A, NL-3707 GL Zeist.

There are also full-time courses in Australia, Austria, Canada, Denmark, Finland, New Zealand, Norway, South Africa and South America.

Information on the many part-time and in-training courses are available through the national Waldorf School organizations. (In Great Britain this is: The Steiner Waldorf Schools Fellowship, Kidbrooke Mansion, Michael Hall, Forest Row, E. Sussex RH18 5JB, www.steinerwaldorf.org.uk) Current lists of schools can also be obtained from them.

NOTES

Foreword
1. See R. Steiner, *A Social Basis for Education*, SSF 1994 (GA 192, lectures of 11 and 18 May and 1 June 1919).
2. R. Steiner, *A Social Basis for Education*, SSF, 1994, lecture of 11 May 1919 (GA 192).
3. See *Steiner Education* magazine (the modern version of *Child and Man* that Francis Edmunds was so closely associated with), Vol. 36, No. 3, 'New Educational Landscapes', by Thomas Stöckli.

Chapter 3
1. H. Poppelbaum, *Man and Animal—Their Essential Difference*, Anthroposophical Publishing Co., London, 1960.
2. This journal is now entitled *Steiner Education*.
3. A.C. Harwood, *The Way of a Child*, Rudolf Steiner Press, London, 1988.

Chapter 5
1. Since this book was written teachers have generally noticed that there are far fewer phlegmatic children than in the past. This may be due to the fast pace of modern life (editor's note).
2. C. von Heydebrand, *Childhood*, Rudolf Steiner Press, London, 1988.

Chapter 6
1. With permission of A.M. Heath & Co., and acknowledgements to Mr Diarmuid Russell.
2. For a modern edition see Soloviev, *The Heart of Reality, Essays on Beauty, Love and Ethics*, University of Notre Dame Press, 2003.
3. With permission of MacMillan & Co.

Chapter 8
1. A college in East Sussex, UK, offering a variety of courses based on Steiner's work.
2. Since this book was written, many new schools have started throughout the world.

Chapter 12
1. In 2003 discussions are now far advanced for the first state-funded Steiner school to open in the UK.

Weblinks

World list of Steiner Schools, available at:
www.waldorfschule.info

Association of Waldorf Schools of North America (AWSNA):
www.waldorfeducation.org

Steiner Waldorf Schools Fellowship (UK):
www.steinerwaldorf.org.uk

European Council for Steiner Waldorf Education:
www.ecswe.org

Alliance for Childhood:
www.allianceforchildhood.org.uk

International Federation of Kindergartens:
www.waldorfkindergarten.org

Online Waldorf Library:
www.waldorflibrary.org

General information and further links:
www.waldorfworld.net